"Women's contributions in the early church have long been over-looked. Pamela Smith's *WomanGifts: Biblical Models for Forming Church* carefully explores the Book of Acts and the epistles to raise up 65 images of women forming church, creating a series of exquisite meditations that lead to powerful prayer and probing questions. Smith speaks heart to heart. She invites a new awareness of women's abilities to evoke church in every age."

Sydney Condray
Author, *Assembled in Christ*

"The early church will come to life in these pages. You will meet women who will gentle you, sometimes challenge you, always make you think. Some of them will show you up; others will show you how. Some feed your heart with quiet faith; some feed your head with surer stuff.

"Pamela Smith is true to her name: She is a Word-Smith; she knows her craft, her Scripture, and obviously knows God's love—firsthand—and knows how to suggest forming today's church, with love foremost."                Isaias Powers, C.P.

Author, *Women of the Gospel*

"Pamela Smith focuses on women's gifts in forming and shaping real church. The book is a series of reflections on Scripture texts, followed by brief prayers and questions for reflection and discussion. As such, it engages the reader in prayer. The format lends itself to reflection, either individually or communally, on the personal and communal implications of the Scripture.

"Those who desire to deepen their prayer and stretch beyond familiar understandings will not be disappointed with this book. With nuanced thought, surprising connections, and poetic language, the author opens up a text to savor."

Margaret Fitzer, S.S.L.
Executive Director, Religious Formation Conference

"Once again Sister Pam Smith offers fascinating insights that touch the hearts of her growing number of readers. With the sensitivity of a poet and the realism of a theologian, she raises our consciousness to a higher level of appreciation for women who helped form the church in biblical times. With spiritual acuteness balanced by emotional warmth, she challenges us to affirm women who are re-forming the church in our own day.

"This book is a must-read, especially for those who have yet to recognize all the gifts women have contributed and are contributing to the church and to the human family at large."

Very Rev. T. Ronald Haney
Author, *Today's Spirituality*

"With *WomanGifts* Pamela Smith favors us with a sequel to her popular *WomanStory*. This time she takes us through the Acts of the Apostles and the Pauline letters, discovering real, breathing women where the rest of us see only strange names. While women serve as her point of departure, her reflections quickly move beyond mere gender.

"Her prayers gently call our own hearts to Scripture-based prayer. Her poetic style, alive with fresh imagery, engages our hearts and our imaginations. I hope the growing number of lay ministers, men and women, will use *WomanGifts* for their own enrichment."

William J. Rademacher
Author, *Lay Ministry*

"Under the gifted guidance of Sr. Pamela, Scripture texts come to life with a freshness no receptive reader can miss. By mining the treasures of ancient yet ever new biblical models—with a special emphasis on "WomanGifts"—she offers us substantial insights into the ongoing formation of church and society.

"This is a book to read and to savor. It echoes with familiar strains while being full of surprises. I foresee its usefulness in the classroom as well as in retreat centers."

Dr. Susan Muto
Author, *Womanspirit*

"Pamela Smith helps her readers to see women as central in the formation of the early church. She not only lifts up those women whose names have been preserved in the scriptures but she reminds us that women are included in all the passages that refer to the life of the church. Women and men who are still forming the church today will find this book of reflections invaluable. *WomanGifts* is truly gift for the church."

Regina Coll, C.S.J.
Author, *Christianity and Feminism in Conversation*

PAMELA SMITH

# WOMAN GIFTS

Biblical Models 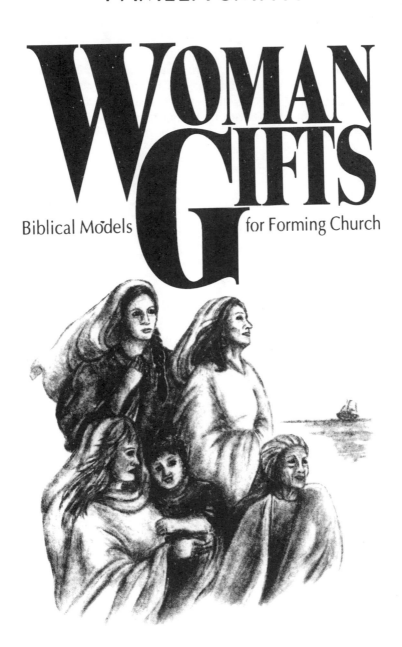 for Forming Church

TWENTY-THIRD PUBLICATIONS
Mystic, Connecticut 06355

## Acknowledgment

All scriptural quotations are from *The Holy Bible: New Revised Standard Version,* © 1989, Division of Christian Education of the National Council of the Churches of Christ in the United States of America; published by Oxford University Press, New York.

**Art by Virginia DeWan, SS.C.M.**

Twenty-Third Publications
185 Willow Street
P.O. Box 180
Mystic, CT 06355
(203) 536-2611
800-321-0411

ISBN 0-89622-572-0
Library of Congress Catalog Card Number 93-60404
Printed in the U.S.A.

For my mother, Elma Russell Smith,
and for Sister Cyrilline

# CONTENTS

# WOMAN GIFTS

# INTRODUCTION

Whenever I drive through Pennsylvania's mountains, rolling along slight inclines into Philadelphia or coasting the hills of evergreen forest amid anthracite region slag piles or scaling Laurel Summit on the road from Altoona to Pittsburgh, I am impressed by the many steeples in the valleys and along the skylines. A multitude of churches mark the history of our farm villages, mining towns, commercialized boroughs, and polyglot cities. And these churches still clearly touch our lives.

Much has changed in the church in my own lifetime. In Catholicism we have rearranged furnishings, titles, ministerial roles, and many other things; we have also reexamined our thinking and reclaimed much of the biblical spirit. With Protestant and Orthodox groups, we have learned to pray together and to celebrate the rich Christian heritage we hold in common.

But we have also discovered that institutional inertia and old prejudices can hold us back, even as the challenge to evangelize and incarnate Christ-in-the-world presses upon us. When I think back to my childhood days in the church, I recall that incense, candlelight, gold, and the delicate lilt of Gregorian chant entranced me as much as the goodness of churchgoers did. But I realize now that what has held me is—and can only be—the person of Christ, encountered in some indescribable ways in himself but also met among the body of gentle people, true believers, women and men who commit themselves to *making* and *remaking* the church. And, in the end, I realize that the making and remaking of the church often has very little to do with the architectural monuments that span the countryside.

### Forming Church Today
When I consider what forms church, what brings people together in the name of Jesus and in a bond of love, I conclude that it happens only in some "official" church quarters and rarely parish-

1

wide or institution-wide. The phenomenon of church always seems to be much smaller, much simpler, and much more local than our technical notion of "local church" (which canonically means the church of a whole diocese). Where I have seen and continue to see church being formed anew is in more intimate, informal, personal places. Prayer groups, Bible study convenings, RCIA journeyers and their companions, Renew clusters, and the faithful remnant who come to ecumenical gatherings—all are making church. So too are retreat groups, summer scholars in religious studies sessions and Bible seminars, communities of sisters and brothers and priests, interfaith coalitions, social justice committees, and all manner of support groups and sharing circles.

The moments when I have most profoundly sensed church in the making and church at work have occurred in settings that allowed for considerable openness of soul, sincere hospitality, comfort with quiet and ease at shared prayer, hunger for knowledge and growth, a patient discontent with the status quo, and an attitude of search. The most alive moments of church have, for me and I suspect for many others, happened amid some brokenness, much reflection, music, laughter, mutual fondness, and an unstuffy seriousness.

The conveners and leaders of what I would like to call *real* church—down-to-earth and close-to-home church—have not necessarily (and maybe not even often) been men. They have been women such as the two creative friends who, in their retirement, sparked the Northwest Indiana Pax Christi group in a Gary, Indiana, church basement. They have been the brains behind lay ministry training programs, catechetical and adult religious education programs, weekend retreats, campus ministry, hospital outreach, and parish renewal. They have been cursillistas and the coordinators of the car-pool groups who get to funeral homes and retirement villages to keep in touch with parish members and their families. They have been the volunteers and the managers of soup kitchens and thrift shops and "love of neighbor" operations. They have been the women who have opened their homes to *ul-*

*treyas* or "Share the Word" groups or charismatic prayer. They have also been the women religious who have moved from autocracy to "shared wisdom" in their government, from rigorous organization to "shared responsibility" in their convent lives, from mysteriousness and formality to theological reflection and more spontaneity in their spiritual style and their prayer. And they are women such as Professor Jamie Phelps who can invite the members of the Catholic Theological Society of America to open their annual convention with a deeply moving, deeply reverent, and very non-academic extended moment of prayer. All these women and others are making church today.

The discussion about whether these or any women should be deacons or priests does not seem to cease. A major point of this book is that women in the early church, like so very many women today, expressed their charisms, endured a certain amount of ecclesiastical and social stress, and led with steady zeal. Without them, it seems hardly possible that we would have the expansive church we have today.

### Content of This Book
When we look back at the church of Acts of the Apostles and the epistles, we find women leading and shaping as well as taking smaller steps. Lydia, Priscilla, and Chloe gather church in their homes. Junia is an "apostle." The daughters of Philip the evangelist are prophets. Phoebe is a deacon. Damaris joins the ranks of upper-crust women and freed servants and slaves who are drawn to the Way. Rhoda answers a door. A few women of that time are negative models, exemplifying the selfishness and distance that unmakes or never even begins to make church: Sapphira, Drusilla, Bernice. I am convinced that the women who are making church today—in parish halls, in prayer corners, in meeting rooms, and in their own homes—can be instructed and inspired by even a quick look at these early-days women.

The format of this book is like that of its predecessor, *WomanStory: Biblical Models for Our Time* (Twenty-Third

Publications, 1992). It assumes that it will be read over a stretch of weeks, probably at the rate of one short chapter per day (or per prayer period). I myself have used the method this book presumes: reading the Scripture slowly and letting it sink in; retelling the story to myself with a focus on the women or the feminine aspect of the sacramental images involved, and adding detail imaginatively to bring the scene to life; offering a short prayer in union with the people of God (thus a "we" prayer rather than an "I" prayer); and, finally, asking some questions that might further examine and apply the Scripture's message.

These chapters spring from my own life experience as well as from my prayer-imaginings. But they are also influenced by reading I have done and discussions I have heard over the years. While this is not strictly a book of theology, I hope it will be found to have solid theological grounding.

## Influences on This Book

I would like to mention several works that have exerted a proximate influence on my thinking and on some of my assumptions. One of the strongest impulses toward a new look at the makeup and identity of the church has continued to come to me from the first encyclical of Pope John Paul II, *Redemptor Hominis*. Its sense of the human person as "the way for the church" is a truly radical concept that deserves years and tomes of reflection. The biblical and historical considerations have been influenced by Frederick Cwiekowski's *The Beginnings of the Church* (Paulist Press, 1988), Florence Gillman's *Women Who Knew Paul* (Liturgical Press, 1992), Mark Allan Powell's *What Are They Saying About Acts?* (Paulist Press, 1991), and Elisabeth Schüssler Fiorenza's *In Memory of Her* (Crossroad, 1983). General considerations of the making and remaking of the church have received a boost from Sally Cunneen's *Mother Church* (Paulist Press, 1991), Vincent Donovan's *Christianity Rediscovered: An Epistle from the Masai* (Fides/Claretian, 1978), *The Church in the Midst of Creation* (Orbis Books, 1989), and William Rademacher's *Lay Ministry* (Crossroad, 1991).

I count among the great blessings of being at Duquesne University the opportunity it has provided for imbibing some of Rademacher's and Donovan's forward-looking, historically rooted church spirit. Both men are exemplary in their thinking and writing as well as in their priesthood. (This acknowledgment will also, I trust, allay any fears that the book reflects any lack of appreciation for men or for ordained priests. My interest here is simply to honor the influential role of women in church-forming and to advance some biblical models for a more profoundly inclusive and collaborative ecclesiology and ministry.)

### Readers of This Book

As with *WomanStory*, I hope that this book serves a wide audience: male and female, multi-denominational, participant and tentative. While anything I write is Catholic in the institutional affiliative sense, I hope it is sincerely *catholic* in speaking to something universal in the human heart: the holy desire for conviction, commitment, and adventure. Above all, I hope *WomanGifts* reinforces and expresses what so many of us who are making church today continue to find: that there is multiform, fascinating life in the body of Christ, and that the Holy Spirit prompts this body, ourselves, into uncanny movement and outflow. May we discover, as the believers highlighted in this book did, that we are led by grace into mission, worship, communion, and surprise.

# The Commission
### (Read Acts 1:1–11)

*". . . You will receive power when the Holy Spirit has come upon you; and you will be my witnesses in Jerusalem, in all Judea and Samaria, and to the ends of the earth." When he had said this, as they were watching, he was lifted up and a cloud took him out of their sight. Acts 1:8–9*

BEFORE THE RISEN RABBI vanished into the sky, he had them mulling over villages and cities that lay far across mountain passes, deserts, seas. People in turbans, furs, straw skirts; people with flowers in their hair, bones in their noses, gold rings around their necks; people who tattooed their stomachs, smoked dry leaves, or shortened their feet: Somehow he had thought of them. And those who had watched him imagined and dreamed.

It was hard to begin a work with goodbye.

It almost seemed as though he had meant that they could keep him only if they went on telling the story and, as they did so, gazed into foreign eyes.

The two odd men—angels, they said—got them back down and busy. He would come again, they promised, in just such cloud and hiding.

They told one another. They told his friends. They foresaw travels and marvelous lands. They wondered where feet and camels and ships might take them. And they thought of the different lines and slants, the shapes and skin tones that might make the human face. They thought of colors and cloth and tents and huts and caves and houses of brick with gardens around them and holes in their roofs. The apostles would very soon go to these spots and meet the ones who gathered in marketplaces and the ones who huddled on hills.

But for now they were waiting, in familiar Jerusalem. Before their travels could begin, someone else was coming: an Advocate and Spirit. She was bringing a gift.

*Lord, let us begin every good thing with a fine trajectory: a remembrance, a present moment, a dream of what can be. It is you we remember; it is you we still heed and hear; it is more of your family we are eager to meet. Give us your good timing and your just-right gifts.*

### QUESTIONS FOR REFLECTION AND DISCUSSION

It was in Antioch that the followers of Jesus were first called "Christian," and it was an Antiochene named Ignatius who first called the church "catholic." What does the universality of the church mean to you? Where have you seen it best expressed?

# An Expectant Time of Prayer
*(Read Acts 1:12–14)*

*Then they returned to Jerusalem from the mount called Olivet. . . . When they had entered the city, they went to the room upstairs where they were staying. . . . All these were constantly devoting themselves to prayer. . . . Acts 1:12–14*

THERE WERE, WITH THE ELEVEN, unnumbered women: Jesus' mother and assorted other relatives and followers who prayed together in that room. They asked questions. When they were tired, they mumbled through old psalms. They remembered this, then that, saying of the prophets. They recalled to one another a word, an action, a sign they had heard or seen before the tomb opened, and then the heavens.

From the women the men learned waiting. Who knew how long till something would be born? From Mary they learned heartened pondering. They learned long silences, and they made spaces for the prayer that was unspeakable.

Though they came together intently, they could not force or hurry anything. They could no more make clarity than they could sift the salt from the Dead Sea. They could no more second-guess God's next surprise than they could catch the sun and hold its fire in bare hands. They sat still for what seemed many days.

"Do you wonder what the prophet meant when he spoke of a new heart?" one of the women finally asked.

The Rabbi's mother nodded her head a few times and faintly smiled.

No one said a blessed thing. And there was yet another long, long pause.

*Lord, give us the grace of patient waiting. Steady us in our haste for definition and direction. Open us, your people, to slow change and eventual revelation.*

## QUESTIONS FOR REFLECTION AND DISCUSSION

It seems that there must always be moments of anticipation, uncertainty, and tiresome preparation before any "wow" event in the spiritual life can happen. In your own life, have you ever experienced a time of waiting when you weren't even sure what you were waiting for, even though you sensed it would be something good? When have you with a group gone through stretches of hard work, doubt, and difficulty before you could see a new day dawn? In the end, how do you evaluate such experiences?

Spiritual writers have spoken of a "night of the senses" and "dark night of the soul" when dismay, befuddlement, and near paralysis seem to overtake us. Why do such phases seem necessary for a life in the Spirit?

# THE DESCENT OF THE SPIRIT
### (Read Acts 2:1–4)

*When the day of Pentecost had come, they were all together in one place.*
*And suddenly from heaven there came a sound like the rush of a violent*
*wind. . . . Acts 2:1–2*

AGAIN THEY WERE PRAYING, the women and the men, when
the Spirit battered them. Then fell like hearth fire on a biting
night. Then soothed like unguent cloth on stretched, strapped
muscle.

She shook the house, this holy visitant, but more so wrought
great strengths in them. It was not so much audacity as certainty
they felt. They began to relax and then rhythmically flex with understanding. They began to be able to think about going out and
talking of all that had happened from the Jordan to the last-sight
mountain. They began to know what of himself their Christ had
let stay. That wind and flame? She became familiar. And steady.
And never left them.

*Your Spirit, Lord, is sometimes sudden and sometimes slow-dawning.*
*Let her wind stir us and her fire warm us. Free us to see, to speak, to rise*
*to action in every season.*

## QUESTIONS FOR REFLECTION AND DISCUSSION
Pentecost has traditionally been called "the birthday of the
church." Do you find that fitting? Explain.

In the encyclical *Dominum et Vivificantem* (On the Holy Spirit in
the Life of the Church and the World), Pope John Paul II em-
phasizes the role of the Spirit as "giver of life," "soul of the
church," and strengthener of the "inner person." When have you

found a hidden strength within yourself that came forth when you needed it? When have you been aware that some idea, impulse, or action in your life was inspired by the Holy Spirit?

How, in recent years, has the church become more aware and expressive of the action of the Holy Spirit? How else might the church call attention to the reality and power of the Spirit?

# THE GIFT OF TONGUES
### (Read Acts 2:5–13)

" . . . In our languages we hear them speaking about God's deeds of power." All were amazed and perplexed, saying to one another, "What does this mean?" But others sneered and said, "They are filled with new wine." Acts 2:11–13

WHEN THEY WENT OUT, they spoke the languages of Cappadocia and Mesopotamia, Egypt and Libya, Arabia and Crete. They would learn Navaho and Swahili. They would master Gaelic and Tuareg, Icelandic and Sanskrit, the accents of mountain people in Appalachia and the Andes, the rhythms of Formosa and Mozambique, the Aleutian Islands and Tibet. They spoke, like Jesus before them, the languages of the heart. The men heard freedom, justice, vision, hope. The children heard welcome, future, affection, and self-respect. The women heard the language of endurance, equality, steadfastness, peacemaking, sisterhood, strength.

Some stood apart and thought them slurred and muddled with whatever mystery or elixir or heart's ease they'd imbibed.

The disciples, meanwhile, began to foresee wild new possibilities—for world, community, belovedness, belief.

They began to know a God who spoke to people as they were, as they could understand, a God whose realm was bigger than they had dreamed.

They could not help but mention it.

Lord God, let us recognize your gift, the gift of you yourself loving us, every and each. And let us spread that gift of love, blessing others, irrepressibly. Let all lands ring with words of your praise.

## QUESTIONS FOR REFLECTION AND DISCUSSION

Who would you consider today to be the ones who most need to hear the news of Christ and a word of love? How would one go about "speaking their language" to get the message across?

# METANOIA
## (Read Acts 2:37–42)

*Peter said to them,"Repent, and be baptized every one of you in the name of Jesus Christ so that your sins may be forgiven; and you will receive the gift of the Holy Spirit. For the promise is for you, for your children, and for all who are far away, everyone whom the Lord our God calls."*

*Acts 2:38–39*

WHEN A GIFT COMES, there must be someone home to take it in her hands or someone who arrives shortly who can find it and open it promptly. But how can one be home or know when to return and go looking? The listeners learned that it took a turning. The women, the men, even the older children would have to look at sin and, about-face, set foot on new paths and undertake new ways. They would have to strip and drench themselves in water. There would be disciples, women and men, who would wade in with them, baptize them in the name of the Father-God and the Messiah-Son and the Spirit-One, and anoint them. These disciples would also guide them as they learned anew to walk and feel at home.

The three thousand of that signal Pentecost were only the first of the many who would hear, believe, reroute, immerse, and pray and praise and tell and tell. They would accept the gift and turn about.

*Generous God, open our hands to receive your Spirit and to treasure the gift of baptism. Open our minds to understand, and help us to follow your paths. Make of our hearts your home. Then let us share your gift, passing on your light and benefit.*

## QUESTIONS FOR REFLECTION AND DISCUSSION
*Metanoia* is the Greek word for a change of mind and heart. In

what ways does Christian faith require us to change our attitudes, values, and life-orientations?

The first baptisms of Christians recorded in Scripture took place quickly. It seems that people had only to hear the Good News, attest that they believed, and present themselves. It happened in a matter of hours or even moments. Why does the church today require a much more lengthy preparation for Christian initiation?

# THE FIRST COMMUNITY
### (Read Acts 2:43–47)

*Day by day, as they spent much time together in the temple, they broke bread at home and ate their food with glad and generous hearts, praising God and having the goodwill of all the people. Acts 2:46*

THE JEWISH WOMEN among them were used to Sabbath prayer, to blessings and food and holy meals, to making worship at home. The Roman women who would later come had their lares and penates, the Greeks their images and myths, and all their sacred words and signs and smells. These followers of the risen Rabbi, the early ones and the later ones who came amid testimonies and house-shakings and new baptism, made homes into synagogues and sanctuaries. They still met at the Temple, knowing now that God held residence not only in the Holy of Holies, on the holy hill, within the sacred walls, but outside too—in their small houses, in their glad groups, in their stirred hearts. They prayed; they pooled their properties; they noticed every need. The women set their tables and joined the men to sing, softly, praise. More and more came to see and take and taste and eat.

*Lord of Sabbath rest and bread, let us celebrate your love and your saving, your provision and your staying with. Increase us as we memorialize your acts on our behalf and mark your presence in our midst.*

## QUESTIONS FOR REFLECTION AND DISCUSSION
One of the well-known strengths of the church in Latin America today is the *communidad de base*, the basic Christian community. At the heart of the movement is prayer and reflection on Scripture from the perspective of the life-situation of the members. Why does such a style of faith-gathering lead inevitably to social and political action as well as to what has conventionally been considered "religious" activity?

# The Prophet, The Servant, Someone's Son

### (Read Acts 3:11–26)

*[Peter said to them:] "And all the prophets, as many as have spoken, from Samuel and those after him, also predicted these days." Acts 3:24*

THEY PREACHED TO EVERYONE about their Messiah-prophet. He had arisen among Moses' people and was a son of the line of Abraham, Isaac, and Jacob. He had come up from water in John's baptism like one taken by the pharaoh's daughter from young Miriam. He was the son of sadnesses and surprise, like Sarah's, Rebecca's, and Leah's sons. He was servant, like Mary, the mother who came and whispered with the disciples in prayer and calmed them in the upper room. Much of his life had been hidden, and his lifeless body had been hidden in a tomb. But that tomb could not keep him. He had risen and given his strength for the frightened, the sinful, the quizzical, the lame.

God had given him glory. The chosen had given him a history. Mary had given them his very life, their brother Christ.

*God, your apostle told the story like one still entranced: how Jesus had been the convergence of promise and long lines. He had a genealogy. Your Messiah was a mother's son as well as the suffering one of Isaiah's song. We cannot second-guess your ways, Almighty, nor miss how extraordinariness can come upon us when we least expect it: from the plainest life-and-death, wake-and-sleep, Hebrew-girl starts.*

## Questions for Reflection and Discussion

In the encyclical letter *Redemptoris Mater* (Mother of the Redeemer, 20), Pope John Paul II credits Mary with being "the first 'disciple' of her Son, the first to whom he seemed to say,

---

17

'Follow me.'" What characteristics of the disciple do you find in Mary?

The pope has also spoken of the importance of Mary's role as an expression of the dignity of women, their equality with men, and their bearing the "image and likeness" of God. In *Mulieris Dignitatem* (On the Dignity and Vocation of Women), he highlights the importance of the fact that "a woman is to be found at the center of this salvific event," the Incarnation (3). He also says that Mary's realization of union with God is the model of all human destiny: "From this point of view, the 'woman' is the representation and the archetype of the whole human race: she represents the humanity which belongs to all human beings, both men and women" (4). For you, how does Mary offer a feminine perspective on the meaning of human life?

In the same apostolic letter, John Paul II reminds us that "the [Vatican] Council has confirmed that, unless one looks to the Mother of God, it is impossible to understand the mystery of the Church, her reality, her essential vitality" (22). In what ways does Mary help us to understand what it means to be church?

# Times To Be Silent, Times To Speak
### (Read Acts 4:18–20)

*[Peter and John retorted:] "We cannot keep from speaking about what we have seen and heard." Acts 4:20*

THE WOMEN, who were used to the outer courts of the temple and synagogue silences, felt compelled to speak. With the men, they had their truth to tell. And the truth was a person who had walked, taught, eaten, drunk, befriended them, gathered them as readily as rabbis gathered disciple-men, been denounced and then crucified, and had risen after he died.

With the community, with Peter and John, they knew that this truth would storm inside them if they held it in. They could not *not* speak. No human force could silence them.

*Lord, when your being wells up within us, let us tell your story. Let us be simple, clear, matter-of-fact, and sure—glad with a glow that is confident in the undeniable strength of your truth.*

## QUESTIONS FOR REFLECTION AND DISCUSSION

In the Second Vatican Council's Dogmatic Constitution on the Church (*Lumen Gentium*), there is a powerful reminder that all the faithful are called to evangelize—to be "powerful heralds" of faith, "announcing . . . Christ by a living testimony as well as by the spoken word" (35). On a day-to-day basis, how do you evangelize?

What is the role of contemplation, prayer, and silence in evangelization?

# A Prayer for Courage
### (Read Acts 4:23–31)

*When they had prayed, the place in which they were gathered together was shaken; and they were all filled with the Holy Spirit and spoke the word of God with boldness. Acts 4:31*

THE COMMUNITY PRAYED to be brash. The women would not be snippy and resentful, nor abrupt or irritable, putting people off. No, they would become solid and tall. They would be both more eloquent and more patient than they had ever been known to be. They were becoming not holy wildfire but the steady, warm blue of eternal flame. Even if they died for the Messiah, even if they made a long procession to Roman arenas or Palestinian hills where townspeople heaved stones, they knew their story would go on. The One who set the stars sparkling and fed the fire of sun would waft a wind across field and city, cool lake and salt sea—across whole expanses of earth. The Abba-God, their Love, would not let their graves seal them off or quiet them down. They had prayed. And they had the undying word of his Servant-Son.

*The quality of courage, God, is not blind faith in our own strength but assurance that you will see us through. We know that your good purposes triumph and your great works never die. Keep us confident and afire as we do your deeds and profess your truth.*

## Questions for Reflection and Discussion

Ernest Hemingway described courage as "grace under pressure." Christians believe that fortitude—enduring courage—is one of the seven gifts of the Holy Spirit. What is your understanding of courage? Who has it? How does it work?

Whom would you select as examples of courageous women?

# KOINONIA: BONDED IN LOVE
## (Read Acts 4:32–35)

*Now the whole group of those who believed were of one heart and soul.*

*Acts 4:32*

BECOMING OF "one heart and soul" took masses of grace and everyone's gifts, the early followers of the Way found. The women brought their conciliatory skills, their keeping of confidences, their experiences of smoothing rough paths and finding other, new means to do things, to speak together, to think. Their gift of "shalom," their skill at give-and-take, and their years of soothing their men, their children, their women relatives, their women friends served them. The Rabbi perhaps had learned it from his mother, this gentling, this talent for highlighting the good, the potential, of persons, this way of carrying an aura of calm. He had noticed each one's needs and attuned his disciples to responding to them, to loosening their grip on their own provisions, just as he had taught them to loosen their grip on their forethoughts, their prejudices, their preconceptions.

The believers gave way to one another, opened their hands, sold their land, turned everything over, all for all.

*Lord, teach us the art of letting go. Let us look more to what we can contribute and what resources we can pool than to our own wants and needs. Gentle us with one another in the back-and-forth of our everyday lives.*

## QUESTIONS FOR REFLECTION AND DISCUSSION

What do you consider the essential gifts for building community (*koinonia*, which in Greek suggests a partnership and a kind of marital union)? Are there "masculine" gifts and "feminine" gifts involved in making community, or are there simply "human" gifts? Are there "natural" gifts and "supernatural" gifts? If so, what are they?

# Mistaken Sapphira
### (Read Acts 5:1–11)

*But a man named Ananias, with the consent of his wife Sapphira, sold a piece of property; with his wife's knowledge, he kept back some of the proceeds, and brought only a part and laid it at the apostles' feet.*

Acts 5:1–2

THERE IS A KIND OF stinginess that smuggles goods away even from God and then straight-facedly denies it. Ananias and Sapphira believed but clung to their security in case there might be, let's say, a later twist to the story, a sapping or scattering of this Jesus' following, an unanticipated need or two or three. It was, they reasoned, common sense and safety, and no one, not even God, could possibly expect them to give over everything.

Sapphira's sudden death, in the midst of a lie, stunned the community to wonder what fractions they, each by each, were also holding in reserve and what possible good any withholdings could come to.

*God, we in your church today are grudging in our giving, and it seems that only a few great saints over these centuries have truly surrendered everything. Teach us to look to the common good and to empty ourselves for our sisters and brothers as well as for you. Help us to see the futility of all our sureties and holdings on. And let us spend ourselves as though we know that all we have is gift.*

## Questions for Reflection and Discussion

Why are miserliness and basic selfishness barriers to community?

Do you think that there is a Sapphira-mentality behind some of our domestic and international problems? If so, explain.

23

# The Healing Touch
### (Read Acts 5:12–16)

*A great number of people would also gather from the towns around Jerusalem, bringing the sick and those tormented by unclean spirits, and they were all cured. Acts 5:16*

BEYOND SOLOMON'S PORCH there were ripples—miracles even. This strange group of believers had healing in them. Rumor brought crowds just to stand near Peter's shadow.

They remembered bowls of warmth and a mother's touch in their childhood illnesses. They recalled the health of sun and the women who had carried them, nursed them, covered them from chill, cooled fever, and made them, it seemed, well. They remembered grandmothers' herbs and remedies, blessings passed on, and soothing words layered with prayer.

This healing was like those memories, but suddener, holier, more. And each one of these Jesus-believers cast some shadow, not of grimness and gray, but of life and well-being, out there past the temple portico.

*Spirit of healing and mother love, enfold us in health and calm. Raise us with our brother, the Son.*

## Questions for Reflection and Discussion
In what sense is *every* Christian called to be a healer?

# THE GREEK-SPEAKING WIDOWS
### (Read Acts 6:1–7)

*Now during those days, when the disciples were increasing in number, the Hellenists complained against the Hebrews because their widows were being neglected in the daily distribution of food. And the twelve called together the whole community of the disciples. . . . Acts 6:1–2*

SOMEONE, AMONG THOSE who were looking to others' needs rather than to their own, noticed inequities and partialities. Someone, among those who were to turn the other cheek, raised objections. These protestations may have been quietly factual or acridly shrill. They may have come from understated hurt or cranky resentment. But someone made her observations and wondered aloud about prejudice. Someone saw the Aramaic and Hebrew-speaking widows better fed and funded, while the Greek-speaking (from the diaspora Jews) embraced the same Jesus, celebrated the same good news, and found their fare was table crumbs. It did not seem right or just to settle for them. Better to challenge the sisters and brothers to even-handedness and honest care— if indeed the Rabbi had called them to be all for all.

Someone's complaints and someone's demands for fair distribution of the goods they shared prompted a new order in this kingdom of mercy, this kingdom of harmony and hope they were striving for. From needy widows with a foreign accent and a worthy gripe, deacons were born. They would speak the word and wait on tables and see that the common resources were justly spent. There would be no classes or castes among them. There would be attention when someone spoke up. And there would be creative response when her words stung. They remembered again and again that Jesus had tried to feed and reverence everyone. There had been no foreigners for him.

*Spirit of Jesus, help us to know when it is timely to speak our peace. Let us be driven not by selfishness but by a truth that frees and makes new things.*

## QUESTIONS FOR REFLECTION AND DISCUSSION

What voices in the church and the world today are calling our attention to inconsistencies and inequities? Are there "have-nots" whose situations we continue to make excuses for or justify?

Compare and contrast the roles of the first deacons with those of today. If a diaconate for women were to be re-inaugurated in Catholicism, would you expect there to be any distinctions between the roles of women deacons and those of men?

# THE SAMARITANS, AFTER THE WOMAN
### (Read John 4:4–42; Acts 8:4–8)

*Philip went down to the city of Samaria and proclaimed the Messiah to them. The crowds with one accord listened eagerly to what was said by Philip. . . . Acts 8:5–6*

THERE HAD BEEN A woman once who had been scoffed by most of the townsfolk for her turnover of men. Then later there had been her well-side story about the Messiah. All this was much before Philip. Some remembered. Something about her story and everything about the Rabbi she had rushed them to meet rang true. Then he had disappeared. But she stayed, much changed. Now and then they had spoken of it. She told them that at the well they had spoken of worship—worship in spirit and truth. The fact that their mountain was not his forebears' mountain seemed not to matter. Wherever shrines or temples were, or whether there were any shrines or temples at all, seemed not to concern him. It was their own stories, their hopes and fears and ambitions and pains and intents, their innermost meanings and secret beliefs—these interested him. That, at least, was what the woman had said and what some few who remembered seemed to attest. When, now and then, someone had asked the woman what actually had happened between them, she spoke of water. She motioned wordlessly and then paused with hands raised and proffered something invisible, as if she could answer them with air. And then she commented abstractedly about what passes and what lasts. She seemed to have learned some secret of love.

When Philip came claiming that her mysterious Messiah and love had died but was still alive, they began to make some sense of it. They began to wonder if they too might draw from her underground tide, her inner stream. And the more they heard, the more they believed.

*Lord of living water and lasting love, continue to teach us in our every-where. Wash us in your word of life, and let us drink deep of your wisdom and care. Stay with us, Lord, and give us reverent pause as we recall, make sense, and are refreshed.*

## QUESTIONS FOR REFLECTION AND DISCUSSION

In missionary efforts, it is understood that a vitally important phase is *praeparatio evangelica*, laying the groundwork for evangelizing. While Acts recounts Philip's mission to Samaria, John 4 tells an earlier story of a Samaritan woman's encounter with Jesus and the testimony she gave her people. Why might her story be an important prelude to the story of Philip's success? What important things might she have been able to reveal about Jesus that Philip perhaps could not?

# CANDACE'S ENVOY
### (Read Acts 8:26–40)

*As they were going along the road, they came to some water; and the eunuch said, "Look, here is water! What is to prevent me from being baptized?" Acts 8:36*

THERE ARE SOME MORNINGS when a smear of yellow turns light pink and whitens clouds in a still-gray sky. Long before dawn a subtle color-play ignites, and one who watches long sees slow kaleidoscope.

South, in Ethiopia, Candace the queen watched sky and sent her treasurer traveling. North, in Jerusalem, Philip the disciple had made his pilgrimage too and set out, with the dawn on his left, to meet the South on the road to Gaza.

The eunuch learned Isaiah and the Lamb of God. He dived into baptismal water and was filled with glee.

More light, more color, streamed across Candace's eastern sky. Her treasurer would have much to tell her, much profit to present.

*Story by story, Lord, you tinge our lives with light. May we listen as your Word is explained and your story told from one to another to another. Open our eyes to the rising bright sky.*

## QUESTIONS FOR REFLECTION AND DISCUSSION

Any number of religious experiences and faith events seem to be happy coincidences, cases of people appearing in the right place at the right time. Do you credit such "accidents" to the Holy Spirit? Have you yourself experienced any such meetings that seemed providential?

Africa today is one of the sites of greatest growth in church membership. Since Christianity clearly made an entry into Africa within decades of the death and resurrection of Jesus, how do you account for the fact that Christianization is only now a strong movement?

# TABITHA RISING
## (Read Acts 9:36–42)

*Now in Joppa there was a disciple whose name was Tabitha, which in Greek is Dorcas. She was devoted to good works and acts of charity. At that time she became ill and died. When they had washed her, they laid her in a room upstairs. Acts 9:36–37*

WHEN TABITHA (called Dorcas) died, the widow disciples wailed their disbelief. They could not picture their new band of believers bereft of her graciousness, wisdom, and good. Tabitha had been the open-handed one, the bountiful maker and giver of cloth and clothes, and the ready receiver of all their griefs. "Not yet," they cried when her body lay elegant and laved. New as they were, they needed her spirit for support. She was a strong exemplar of the Way, and there had been so little time for her to mentor. The Rabbi had raised, they knew, a little girl, a widow's son, and his entombed good friend. He surely could call her forth from the distance of death to minister more to them. Until at least they could better learn her good deeds and their sacred source. Until perhaps they could discern the manner of the Lord's coming and coming again.

When Peter laid hands and prayed her to awake, open-eyed and glad to smile on them, they gently rocked. They swayed with slow peace at the life that was lent them. They made slow dance at the claims they could make on this Jesus-God.

*No matter how alive your life is, Lord, there are those we cannot seem to live without. Give us the human contacts, the guidance and goodness we need, for long enough. We learn your way by seeing and receiving. And we learn with grateful hearts.*

QUESTIONS FOR REFLECTION AND DISCUSSION

Who in your life would you rate as indispensable mentor or mentors?

# THE ANTIOCHENES
## (Read Acts 11:19–26)

*. . . On coming to Antioch, [they] spoke to the Hellenists also, pro-
claiming the Lord Jesus. The hand of the Lord was with them, and a
great number became believers and turned to the Lord. Acts 11:20–21*

SOME NIGHTS WHEN the women of Antioch dropped off to
sleep, the stars seemed to sing. There had been cosmic waiting
and then a child who had grown to be a rabbi. Some called him
brother; some, prophet and healer; some called him friend; many,
messiah; and others, king and even divine son. Whoever of
these—and maybe all of these—he might have been, they began
to see that he was changing everything. Those who told the news
brought serenity and sense. They spoke of triumph and lastingness—triumph over death, lastingness of love. They brought
them together, Jews and Greeks, Cypriots and Antiochenes, staid
traditionalists and wildfire enthusiasts, as family, as brothers and
sisters of this one who had mounted the sky.

They called him the anointed one, the Christ. And those who
heard music at starlight and later lilted with the rise of the Syriac
sun were called a new name: Christian.

*Lord Christ, sing to us softly your lullabies and reveilles. Attune us to
universe harmony and the rhythms of history. You orchestrate it all. In
chorus and responsory, let us praise your name.*

## QUESTIONS FOR REFLECTION AND DISCUSSION
Is there a difference between being Christian by birth and cul-
ture and Christian by freely chosen adult commitment? Is there a
sense in which we need to be "born again" to be truly Christian?

In Antioch the followers of Jesus were first identified by others
as "Christians." What does it imply for you or anyone else to
claim the identity of Christian today?

# FAMINE-FEEDERS
## (Read Acts 11:27–30)

*At that time prophets came down from Jerusalem to Antioch. One of them named named Agabus stood up and predicted by the Spirit that there would be a severe famine over all the world; and this took place during the reign of Claudius. The disciples determined that according to their ability, each would send relief. . . . Acts 11:27–29*

THE WOMEN FOREVER had made table-fare spread so that all who hungered could eat. When famine came to Judea, the Antiochenes packed parcels of food for their Christian kin. Breaking bread was not just remembrance of a Passover night in an upper room; it was, for them, the very call of Peter: Feed my lambs, tend my sheep. The women knew that all who could *should* feed; that any who wanted *should* be tendered some of what the better-fed had to eat.

*Jesus, breaker of bread, keep us alert to the hunger of our world. Show us a way to regard no one as foreign and all as cousin, kindred, friend. Give us imagination and effectiveness as we seek ways to make for simple, satiating, worldwide banquet. And help us to repent our gluttony and waste.*

## QUESTIONS FOR REFLECTION AND DISCUSSION

Christians and Westerners in general are usually generous responders to appeals for disaster and famine relief. How do you explain the slowness or ineffectiveness of response to some situations of famine in recent times? What do you feel might need to be done to get goods to those who need them more quickly and more directly?

Erecting and supporting soup kitchens, shelters, thrift shops, and the like are among the relief efforts that church groups and charitable organizations have undertaken in the face of poverty and homelessness. Aside from these more or less institutional approaches, is there anything that individuals can do to personalize outreach to people in need?

# THE MOTHER OF JOHN MARK
### (Read Acts 12:6–12)

*As soon as Peter realized [that he had been freed from prison], he went to the house of Mary, the mother of John whose other name was Mark, where many had gathered and were praying. Acts 12:12*

JOHN MARK'S MOTHER made a first house-church. Peter came there when the chains and prison gates sprang open for him. Hers was a house of company and prayer. The disciples banded together there in grief and joy, in intercession and praise. They were poised in silence awaiting the latest word. The mother made space for them and ease. She cooled their thirst, toweled their feet, cushioned their sitting, and waited in whisper and psalm with them. Peter could count on her hosteling and their attention.

John Mark's mother Mary made holy ground there, in her house.

*When your Spirit would speak to our hearts, Lord, we need our sacred places, our quiet hideaways to rest and think and pray. We need our corners for confab and worship. We thank you for the holy homes and centers and meeting rooms that have given us sites to be church.*

## QUESTIONS FOR REFLECTION AND DISCUSSION

We know historically that the "house church" was the typical gathering place for the early Christians. What would be the advantages of such a church? In an age of megaparishes, what are some ways that people have found to downsize their experience of church?

# RHODA THE SERVANT
### (Read Acts 12:13–19)

*On recognizing Peter's voice, she was so overjoyed that, instead of opening the gate, she ran in and announced that Peter was standing at the gate. They said to her, "You are out of your mind!" But she insisted that it was so. Acts 12:14–15*

JAILBREAKS MAKE FOR a frenzy. Rhoda was so flustered at the arrival of Peter and the mere sound of his speaking that she rushed with news and left him locked outside. Freedom gushed from Rhoda and then flabbergasted laughter as Peter stood enshrined in doorway. When they collected themselves and ushered him in, Rhoda was gaffed and giggling. They were embarrassed at their brash dismissal of her truth. Peter, meanwhile, spoke of mirage and angelmen and then the sudden alley where he came to himself, unbarred and unchained. Rhoda spoke of the jumble of ghost-thoughts and incredulous joy she had had before she could trust her hearing. The others confessed their nasty old skepticisms. Whoever the liberators had been who had loosed Peter, the disciples and Rhoda knew that they themselves were not angels yet and might not ever be. Their excitements and their depressions could overtake them. But for now, there were practical matters to attend to. Give the man a meal, stealth him away, play dumb, wait a few days, don't laugh or look too knowing if soldiers come. Rhoda withdrew all these things into her startled heart. She would ponder this night for weeks to come but register nothing but calm. She would simply answer knocks and open doors. Another time would come.

*God of grand openings and small apertures of common sense, give us the gifts of attention and prudence. Help us to keep our wits about us and to believe in the truth of our gifts and guests. Stay with us in moments both of delight and of stress.*

## QUESTIONS FOR REFLECTION AND DISCUSSION

The opening door can symbolize many things: hospitality, opportunity, revelation, discovery. In your own religious-spiritual history, who have been some women (even those whose roles might have seemed "unimportant") who have opened doors for you?

# WOMEN FOR, WOMEN AGAINST
### (Read Acts 13:44–52)

*[The unbelieving Antiochenes] incited the devout women of high stand-*
*ing and the leading men of the city, and they stirred up persecution*
*against Paul and Barnabas, and drove them out of their region. Acts*
*13:50*

PAUL AND BARNABAS began to know the power of women.
There were women, Gentile and Jewish, who listened, mulled
over the message, assented, and believed. They saw light, became
it, and carried the light to their towns.

There were women sympathetic with the silencers too, women
of clout and cleverness who unsettled Pisidian Antioch. Paul and
Barnabas dusted their feet. Those women grew cataracts across
their souls.

*Lord, remove the darkness from our hearts and the shades from our eyes.*
*Dawn upon us so that we ourselves may be enlightened and may bear*
*your light.*


## QUESTIONS FOR REFLECTION AND DISCUSSION
In some ways, persecution from outside, prejudice on the part
of those from whom we expect it, is relatively easy to accept.
Persecution from inside our faith community or prejudice on the
part of people we would expect to be receptive is difficult and
wearing to confront. How do we know when to keep making efforts to move the group and when to abandon our attempts and
move on? When is it "Christian" to leave people in their narrow-
ness?

# LOIS AND EUNICE
## (Read Acts 16:1–3; 2 Timothy 1:5)

*I am reminded of your sincere faith, a faith that lived first in your grand-mother Lois and your mother Eunice and now, I am sure, lives in you.*

2 Timothy 1:5

THERE IS A FAITH that passes from mothers and grandmothers, from second cousins and great aunts. The children might hold, in their earliest memories, the sight and sound of them at their pieties. Or perhaps they recall a special tranquility. Or perhaps they remember an uncanny knack for asking the right question, soothing the tender wound, noting the need of someone down the street, warming them before sleep, kissing them into their days and their dreams, sensing the secret tears of anyone who weeps. They may have taught their daughters and sons, grandchildren and cousins, nieces and nephews in story and song. They may have hoisted and hustled them off to worship and rallying round. Or they may have brought news to them quietly, after they came home from grown-up gatherings.

We do not know whether Eunice and Lois said much or little, hauled young Timothy along, or let him simply be tucked in by the spirit that suffused the room when they came from preaching and prayer. However it happened, something about them urged their Timothy on—into the arms of the Lord, into a community of believers. Into a vigor of action. Into a faith that passed on and on.

*Spirit of enthusiasm and subtle influence, permeate us. Travel through us—by word, by deed, by implication—from generation to generation.*

## QUESTIONS FOR REFLECTION AND DISCUSSION

The church has long taught that the family is the basic unit of society, the "principal school of the social virtues which are necessary to every society," and the site of people's "first experience of a well-balanced human society and of the church" (Vatican II, Declaration on Christian Education, 3). Who in your family stands out as influential in your own faith-life and development?

For many people today, family is far from an experience of "first church." How can Christians reach out and help create a true sense of "family," particularly for those who have come from negative, disruptive, or abusive situations?

# LYDIA THE MERCHANT
### (Read Acts 16:11–15, 40)

*A certain woman named Lydia, a worshiper of God, was listening to us; she was from the city of Thyatira and a dealer in purple cloth. The Lord opened her heart to listen eagerly to what was said by Paul. When she and her household were baptized, she urged us, saying, "If you have judged me to be faithful to the Lord, come and stay at my home."*

*Acts 16:14–15*

LIKE MANY OF THE FIRST Christians, Lydia may have been a freed woman. Luke says that she was devout, a worshipper of God whose heart was readily widened at Paul's words. She made, with her friends, a synagogue at a stream. On weekdays, she vended purple goods and cloth, the color of emperors and patricians. That Sabbath, when Paul came softly speaking, she laid carpet and hung banners in her soul for his king. She and the women donned new dress, baptismal white, and left the purple borders to the well-to-do and other royalties. When Lydia opened her home too, Paul stayed. He taught the women at the river bank, broke open the word, broke bread, and broke the boundaries of their classes and stations. Soon their kin came too. When Lydia's dwelling housed Paul—and then sheltered him after prison—it seemed that he, rather than she or her friends, was the servant lately freed. And he treated her as if she were benefactor, patron, aristocrat, queen.

*Lord, you give nobility and dignity to us all. The little you ask is that we open wide our hearts and believe. Help us to receive your Word with the graciousness of gentle empresses, and then impel us to give your goods away with the lavish detachment of slaves.*

## QUESTIONS FOR REFLECTION AND DISCUSSION
The fact that Lydia was already a religious person, someone

who revered God before she ever met Paul is pointed out in this scriptural account. In what sense would it be *hard* to "convert" someone who already has firm religious convictions? In what circumstances might it be *easy* to lead such a person to see religion in a whole new light?

According to Florence Gillman, Lydia is "Paul's first convert on European soil." What significance might that have?

# A SLAVE GIRL DELIVERED
(Read Acts 16:16–18)

*One day, as we were going to the place of prayer, we met a slave girl who had a spirit of divination and brought her owners a great deal of money by fortune-telling. While she followed Paul and us, she would cry out....*

Acts 16:16–17

A GIRL COULD GIVE voice to a Python-sprite and an oracle. It was a matter of loosing sounds in her head and a hundred suspicions, a thousand superstitions, around her. She made for dazzle and fear.

When they prayed over her, the bombast and babble quelled. Her spirit was calmed, and she was well.

*Deliver us, O Father-Mother of our Christ, from every cause of chaos. Give solace and stillness to our souls so that we may hear one sound clearly: the sound of your steady truth. You are our good fortune.*

## QUESTIONS FOR REFLECTION AND DISCUSSION

We find "deliverance" churches in the "ghetto" areas of some of our cities. In the apostolic age, deliverance from sorcery and demons was a concern. What are the demons today that people might feel the greatest need for deliverance from?

Anyone who was catechized in Baltimore Catechism days knows that consulting fortune tellers and astrological charts with some degree of credulity was considered a sin against faith. Why would such things (as well as the slave girl's soothsaying) be considered a denial of God's providence and freedom? Why is Christianity generally reluctant to put stock in anyone's private "revelations" or predictions?

# Prominent Women
## of Thessalonica and Beroea
### (Read Acts 17:1–4, 10–12)

*Many of them therefore believed, including not a few Greek women and men of high standing. Acts 17:12*

NOT THAT THE PROMINENCE mattered. But so many of the converts had been destitute Jews or outcast widows, Roman slave girls, Gentiles recently freed, small-time dyers and tentmakers and merchants. A collection, in short, of women and men of the sort likely to be labeled riff-raff by those with high-class profiles, impeccable pedigrees, and abundant jewels. So it seemed at least worth mentioning that some of those who were intrigued by the new Way and embraced it were elegant women, prosperous, influential, well thought of. The Christians, their prophets and speakers, embraced them. And their inelegant, unprosperous, non-influential women, we may surmise, took Thessalonica's and Beroea's ladies to water, unclothed them, and poured baptism all over them.

It was, of course, another sort of miracle: that women so comfortable and cared for and highly regarded that they could afford to be aloof and blasé were moved to let their whole history and social station be stripped and washed away by a mere acquaintance with the one whom more and more were naming Lord and Christ.

It seemed not to matter to them, whether ingenue or grande dame, that their lives might break like Christian bread and spill into the humblest and most beggarly cups like Christian wine.

The chroniclers of those early times found it at least a trifle remarkable. Even if phenomena swirled about them everywhere.

*Savior and Remaker, set us on your path today and steady us with cer-*

*tainty, so that when we find ourselves, in faith, out of step and out of fashion in our society we will continue in your narrow way.*

## QUESTIONS FOR REFLECTION AND DISCUSSION

In what ways might the lifestyle of the rich and the super-rich, the lifestyle of celebrities, be in serious conflict with the way of Christianity?

What is the risk to the life of the church when it attempts to accommodate uncritically the prominent and well-to-do?

# NEWSMONGERS OF ATHENS AND DAMARIS
### (Read Acts 17:21, 32–34)

*Now all the Athenians and the foreigners living there would spend their time in nothing but telling and hearing something new. . . . When they heard of the resurrection of the dead, some scoffed; but others said, "We will hear you again about this." Acts 17:21, 32*

SOMETIMES WE HUMANS weave through streets and stubbled alleyways of mind. Sometimes we curve with question marks of why. It was clear to the Athenians that we breathe and need, that things happen to us and we stir, that we move and change, that we are sameness and surprise. News came of gods on far heights having petty rivalries, skirmishes, outright bloodthirsty fights. Word arrived of councils and orgies. It was said that there were daughter gods, son gods, and a high god. There were cousin gods and demi-gods born of couplings with mortals. No one could verify the rumors of their goings on. Meanwhile the stars fell into shapes in the sky-twins, animals, heroic figures. And the Athenians wondered if these, as they shifted with the passage of the seasons—if these, with the meanderings of planets and the phases of the moon, might not have to do with the world of human fortune.

When Paul came with word of still another phenomenon, it made some sense to a few of them. There were unnameable forces they had fleetingly felt, and they held their dread of death, even amid their pantheon of gods and goddesses. There was something more gentle, something better, in Paul's message than in the other stories they had heard. He had a more sensible God, one more worthy, it seemed, of worship.

Some yearning in them awoke to the possibility of an immortal mortal. And something was piqued by the thought of one who might have taken pain lovingly, forgiven without vengefulness, and spoken, to the unsettled soul, peace.

Damaris, with Dionysius and others, had puzzled over so many things. Paul's persuasive presence and his new thought led them, at least, to stay by him and not wait till some elusive later time. He offered, they believed, so much more than sacrifices on an empty altar to a nameless deity only vague poets could sing.

*God of knowing and unknowing, alert us to your latest word. Dispel our fears and inspire our dreams as you lead us in the ways of hope. Be near to us, O Ever-Real.*

## QUESTIONS FOR REFLECTION AND DISCUSSION

The woman Damaris was among those who attached themselves to Paul and listened carefully to his word. Their believing was inspired by their active listening. What situations and forces in our midst today can assist our "holy" listening? What personal habits and behaviors can render us wisely attentive?

# THE TENTMAKING TEAM:
## PRISCILLA AND AQUILA
### (Read Acts 18:1–4, 18–19, 24–29; Romans 16:3–5;
### 1 Corinthians 16:19–20; 2 Timothy 4:19)

*. . . Paul left Athens and went to Corinth. There he found a Jew called Aquila, a native of Pontus, who had recently come from Italy with his wife Priscilla, because Claudius had ordered all Jews to leave Rome. Paul went to see them, and, because he was of the same trade, he stayed with them, and they worked together—by trade they were tentmakers.*

*Acts 18:1–3*

FROM ROME TO CORINTH to Ephesus and possibly back to Rome, Priscilla and Aquila went bearing tidings, explaining the Way, gathering church in their home. With Paul they made tents. With each other, in partnership, they built up the gangly, sprawling body of Christ. They sent kisses to Rome and shared wisdom with preaching Apollos. They squandered themselves at the Spirit's behest and risked their lives for wandering Paul.

Across borders and in tent shops, Priscilla spoke what she knew. Aside, on the streets, she imparted sage counsel. In her own quarters she made hostel for the Lord's sisters and brothers, apostles, and guests. She prayed, reflected, offered bread, filled and refilled the cup of life.

Tents make safe shelter and fine nomadic shrines. Wherever Priscilla the tentmaker went, there was haven, holy of holies, heavenly home.

*Spirit of good tidings and growing things, draw us into communion with one another. Help us to carry community wherever we go. Make of our hearts safe home, and urge us to spend ourselves unstintingly for greatness and gospel.*

## QUESTIONS FOR REFLECTION AND DISCUSSION

In Catholic circles, it is not unusual to encounter wife-and-husband teams in religious education, marriage preparation programs, natural family planning training, Eucharistic ministry, music ministry, and youth ministry. In Protestant churches, spouses jointly minister in many ways, including, sometimes, serving as co-pastors of their parishes. Priscilla (Prisca) and Aquila were considered apostolic "co-workers," missioners, catechists, and leaders of house churches in several locales. How, in this age of increasing numbers of "priestless" parishes, might you expect Catholics to respond to having a married couple as co-administrators of their parish? How would you respond?

In the early church, the lines of ministry and authority for the service of the word and "table fellowship" were not clearly drawn. Whether or not Priscilla presided over eucharistic meals is probably impossible to learn. She clearly had, however, a dominant role in the house churches associated with her name. How would you picture religious instruction and liturgical celebration going on in such churches?

# At Miletus, A Wave Goodbye

*(Read Acts 20:17–38)*

*When he had finished speaking, he knelt down with them all and prayed. There was much weeping among them all; they embraced Paul and kissed him, grieving especially because of what he had said, that they would not see him again. Then they brought him to the ship.*

*Acts 20:36–38*

LETTING GO OF ONE we have relied on to lead us can be fraught with insecurity and pain. The body seems to depend on a shoulder or biceps, one might say, for its flourishing. The group seems to depend on its most experienced or most certain or most articulate member. So the women, the children, the men of Christian Miletus were toward Paul. As he departed for Jerusalem, they feared he was headed toward death. And death, despite the depth of their resurrection faith, might leave them even more bereft. They could not hold back tears, embraces, kisses. The women waved and waved after the ship. The children jumped on casks and dockside cargo to see, all the while wondering if he could hear their goodbye hollering. The men crossed their arms, turned away, let their eyes mist, scratched their beards in puzzlement.

The good of it all, in the end, was that they learned the power that stayed with and burned within them. The men found ways to pray their silent pain and knew the Spirit's consolation. The children realized that there were, for them, in Christ, adventure, promise, and faraway words to speak. The women came to know their inner wisdom and greeted graciously their divine-inspired gifts. In Jerusalem, church would go on with Paul. In Miletus, it could and did go on without him.

*Giver of everyone's gifts, guide us into confidence as we keep your word and make your Way. We have no greatness apart from a greatness of*

---

*faith. You, God, inflate and send us (like wind in sails) or signal and move us (like mind to muscle and limb). We thank you that, left to ourselves, we find that we are never merely on our own.*

## QUESTIONS FOR REFLECTION AND DISCUSSION
Describe any occasion on which you yourself have experienced or seen in action the grace that moves people to carry on after the loss or departure of a charismatic leader. What happens to people when they realize that they *can* go on and are advancing?

# THE WIVES OF TYRE
### (Read Acts 21:1–6)

*We came in sight of Cyprus; and leaving it on our left, we sailed to Syria and landed at Tyre. . . . We looked up the disciples and stayed there for seven days. Through the Spirit, they told Paul not to go on to Jerusalem. When our days there were ended, we left and proceeded on our journey; and all of them, with wives and children, escorted us outside the city.*

*Acts 21:3–5*

THE MEN WHO USUALLY stood, the women who prayed in back of the men, the children who whispered in lisps on their mothers' laps, all dropped to their knees on open beach.

They had pleaded with Paul not to go on to the peril of Jerusalem. They implored their God in Christ that everything good would not be undone.

The women of Tyre, like the women clustering into discipleship in so many places, were learning to stand tall. They were learning to lift their faces to the sky with confidence, to raise hands in readiness for showers of God's gifts. They blessed the apostle. They let sand grind against their knees and sandaled feet. They let drifts of dune in their folds of skirt and hem.

They carried home a commitment that stretched from Miletus to Ptolemais, from Jerusalem to Rome. They more and more saw that they would be stretched themselves from sky to sand; that there would be both pain and glory in the soul-vault from Tyre to earth's ends.

*Spirit of caution and Spirit of risk, expand our horizons and multiply our gifts. We give all to you for worldwide benefit.*

## QUESTIONS FOR REFLECTION AND DISCUSSION

The disciples of Tyre had a certain caution. They enjoined Paul not to walk directly into the jaws of danger. Similar stories are told today of warnings from families, friends, religious communities that might perhaps have spared some member, amiga, relative from seizure as a hostage or even from assassination. How do we explain the fact that individuals sometimes embark on missions that they know threaten their lives? How can we support those who do go? How would we recognize it if we were so called?

Mother Teresa of Calcutta has one mission style; the women martyred in El Salvador had another. What mission style do you imagine that you would adopt if you were laboring amid an impoverished, oppressed population?

# THE DAUGHTERS OF PHILIP
## THE EVANGELIST
### (Read Acts 21:7–9; 1 Corinthians 12:4–11)

*The next day we left and came to Caesarea; and we went into the house*
*of Philip the evangelist, one of the seven, and stayed with him. He had*
*four unmarried daughters who had the gift of prophecy.* Acts 21:8–9

A CLARITY OF READING and a clarity of speaking some aspect
of the mind of God possesses prophets. Perhaps the daughters of
Philip felt as though their lips had been touched with fiery coals.
Perhaps they felt called even before birth by a God who could
dupe them. Perhaps they had seen dry bones live. Or perhaps,
like Huldah of old, they simply had grasped the ordinances, stat-
utes, demands of an inner law, inscribed by God on human
hearts.

However their gift had come, the same for each or differently
and one by one, these four women listened to wind, watched sky,
heard the secret longings of those around them, and saw through
to where God stood. They gave God, from time to time, a woman's voice.

*Spirit of all knowledge and understanding, all truth, give us clear vision*
*and resonant voice. Let us see you and speak you. And let us celebrate*
*too those who perceive and express you more pristinely than we do.*

## QUESTIONS FOR REFLECTION AND DISCUSSION
How do you understand prophecy in the Old Testament sense?
Is there anything new or different in New Testament prophecy?

In charismatic groups one can often find individuals who are
said to have the gift of prophecy. What sort of "prophecies" are
delivered in these groups? What is the test of their authenticity?

# PAUL'S SISTER
## (Read Acts 23:12–23)

*Now the son of Paul's sister heard about the ambush; so he went and gained entrance to the barracks and told Paul. Paul called one of the centurions and said, "Take this young man to the tribune, for he has something to report to him." Acts 23:16–17*

SHE, LIKE PAUL, was raised a Pharisee—loyal to the law and particular about purifications. She also knew the sacredness of family bonds and blood. She and her son may or may not have been persuaded of the wisdom of Paul's Way. But they knew the demands of justice, the heinousness of trickery, the guilt of a foreseen assault on one's own kin. They knew the evil of silent consent and sitting still. Paul's sister had taught her son well. He spoke the rumor, sounded alarm, and spared an uncle from assassination. He broke the twisted confreres' fast and kept forty men's weapons unbloodied, forty men's fists unswollen and clean. Neither Paul's sister nor he could prevent conspirators' malice, but they could bar the tortuous ways of the human heart from triumphing. Perhaps the woman and the nephew themselves did not know altogether why.

*Help us, Lord, know when to be silent and when to speak, when to keep mum and when to alert. Preserve our love for freedom, fairness, and family.*

## QUESTIONS FOR REFLECTION AND DISCUSSION

This passage contains the only New Testament reference to Paul's sister. In many ways it seems that the new Christians, in whatever community he visited, were the ones Paul considered family. When do we find ourselves in need of "adopting" a new "family" for moral support? How do we balance our connections with this new "family" to our relationships with our family of origin?

We can readily imagine Paul's sister and nephew being moved to intervene on his behalf without any interest in or concern for his newfound faith. We can also imagine their having been drawn to the Christian Way and thus feeling a double urgency about Paul's well-being. Would it make any difference in the message of this scriptural passage if Paul's sister and nephew were believers or unbelievers?

# DRUSILLA THE PRINCESS
*(Read Acts 24)*

*Some days later when Felix came with his wife Drusilla, who was Jewish, he sent for Paul and heard him speak concerning faith in Christ Jesus. And as he discussed justice, self-control, and the coming judgment, Felix became frightened and said, "Go away for the present; when I have an opportunity, I will send for you." Acts 24:24–25*

DRUSILLA, WITH HER uncircumcised husband (and a first one still alive somewhere, left impotent in her walking away), met Paul. His words and his Way left her unscathed. But she and Felix did at least let Paul mention the Christ, the moral life, human destiny, and resurrection. For the moment they were uneasy. But the simplest thing was to leave Paul jailed and to pass him on to a successor.

Drusilla and Felix, governor in Caesarea, left Paul's case unclosed. He was perhaps a bother. Though something—an openness to bribery at least—led Felix to call him out from time to time to talk. Drusilla also heard. We do not know whether later, when the mountain lava washed over her, she had a moment's remembrance. The empire, to her mind, was bustling and full of novelty. For Drusilla, Paul was just another fanatic who could not make peace with things as they were nor fill his days with trite little pleasures. He was one of those who held to some notion of how life might be better and how something, amid much nothingness, might last. Drusilla looked on and wondered what way, what ploy, what fad or rage might be next. He spoke of someone she had not desired or dreamed.

*Lord, let us at least lay out the simplest map of your Way for those we meet. Let us moderately hope. But help us not to lose heart if we face the blank stare, the ho-hum, a deafness. You, in the end, must fuel and impel. We can only suggest to others how they might better travel.*

## QUESTIONS FOR REFLECTION AND DISCUSSION

Florence Gillman ranks Drusilla and Bernice, both daughters of Herod Agrippa I, among those who met Paul, heard him, and were unaffected. She also recounts the legend that Drusilla and a son were swallowed up in an eruption of Vesuvius. Drusilla comes across in history as an opportunist, one whose Jewish heritage was incidental to her. How do we account for the fact that there are so many Drusillas, people who live amid religious surroundings, hear God's word, meet good people, but remain uninfluenced?

# PRINCESS BERNICE
### (Read Acts 25:13—26:32)

*Agrippa said to Paul, "Are you so quickly persuading me to become a Christian?" Paul replied, "Whether quickly or not, I pray to God that not only you but also all who are listening to me today might become such as I am—except for these chains." Then the king got up, and with him the governor and Bernice and those who had been seated with them; and as they were leaving, they said to one another,"This man is doing nothing to deserve death or imprisonment." Acts 26:28–31*

BERNICE SWEPT IN with husband after husband, lover after lover, and a little hint of incest. When she met Paul, it was during one of her times of rule with the beloved brother.

Paul's Rabbi Jesus had spoken of the wealthy and the needle's eye. He had enjoined his disciples too to let be weeds and wheat. Bernice was no disciple. Far from observant of any law, she had only a nodding acquaintance with piety. She was, at times, political, but over all she pleased no one more than herself. She did, however, notice this Paul. He deferred to her brother, was polite and even reverent to her. She heard the long story of his Pharisee life, his early persecutions of the followers of the Nazarene, his eerie experience on the Damascus road, his transformation.

With her brother, she had to admit that there was something gripping in his tale. And so she and Herod Agrippa II listened. Nothing perhaps would come of it. But they recognized sincerity and conviction when they saw them. And they knew innocence, no matter how far or long ago it might have been from them. They knew that Paul deserved no condemnation, was no criminal, no insurrectionist. Perhaps he was a mystic. Or, they mused, perhaps he was the victim of a persuasive delusion.

It would seem that Paul left her, in the end, momentarily moved but unchanged over the long term. She ruled with her brother and stayed at his side whatever way she wished to. Later she cozied close to Titus, selling out to Rome. She languished in rumor and scandal and seems to have become laughingstock when she was near-miss for empress.

But for the time with Paul, she was good enough, and just enough, to judge that he should go free. She saw no sin nor crime in his religiosity.

*Lord, at times we find ourselves entrapped—by social setting, by our own desires and needs, by the clout we seek, by our own sad patterns. Free us, Lord, so that we can respond to the freedom you offer. And clear our minds sufficiently that we can honor the truthseeker when we meet him or her.*

## QUESTIONS FOR REFLECTION AND DISCUSSION

It seems that many of us are capable of trading a godly freedom away for a rather shabby love . . . and another . . . and another. How do we recognize when we are settling for less than the best, less than what is even good for us? How do we search ourselves to learn why?

Had Paul not appealed to the emperor, Acts tells us, he might have been set free at Caesarea Philippi—and thus missed his Roman house arrest and execution (and also an important mission). Do you see Agrippa and Bernice as pawns of fate? Do you see Paul as victim? Would "God's will" have been done whether or not Agrippa and Bernice were converted by Paul? (You might want to check into some of the differences among Christians about the idea of "predestination.")

# SOME JEWISH WOMEN OF ROME
### (Read Acts 28:17–28)

*After they had set a day to meet with [Paul], they came to him at his lodging in great numbers. From morning until evening he explained the matter to them, testifying to the kingdom of God and trying to convince them about Jesus, both from the law of Moses and from the prophets. Some were convinced by what he had said, while others refused to believe. So they disagreed with each other. . . . Acts 28:23–25*

WHEN THE MEN CAME home edgy about the odd ideas of Messiah and the pointed usages of Isaiah they had heard, the women simply kept house around their muttering and agitation. The women paused to listen when the men who had gone to hear Paul would grudgingly extend a word of explanation. When moments of calm and musing seemed to come over them, some of the mothers, sisters, wives probed further with questions.

Might there not be some merit in verifying this story? Might it not be plausible that a Messiah, like the prophets, should die in torment? Could it not be that the God of all creation could raise someone from the dead? Might not the message be more about hope and light and new life than about the shame of crucifixion, the uncleanness of bloodshed?

Occasionally in their hearts, though next to never with their voices, some of these women wondered. They kept watch for the slightest signs that some of the men were bothered by these questions too. But in those who had wrapped their manhood in prayer shawls there was much fight and stubbornness. These were the traits that kept them, in the environs of raw and raucous Rome, tzaddiks and observant. And in the women who had wrapped their lives around observant, certain men, there was much reluctance. A few of them at least resolved that if an opening should come, they would ask and press and ask some more.

*God of the good, the pious, the settled and sure, open us to the occasional shakeup. Prepare our minds and hearts for the metanoia that can receive new thoughts, believe new ways, relax in the face of the surprises you still have in store for your church.*

## QUESTIONS FOR REFLECTION AND DISCUSSION

What fears, what insecurities, might hold us back today from asking uncomfortable questions, challenging fixed concepts, shaking up someone else's concept of God?

Many people, religious people included, find change threatening. What shifts in teaching, approach, or action have you noticed evoking puzzlement or even hostility in your own experience of church?

What new ideas or new presentations of God might you be uncomfortable with? (God as woman, God as homeless, God as minority, God as disabled, God as oppressed, God as devastated Earth? God as a conglomerate of the images held by Christians, Buddhists, Hindus, Muslims?)

# THE WELCOMED
(Read Acts 28:28–31; 2 Corinthians 4:6–7)

*"Let it be known to you then that this salvation of God has been sent to*
*the Gentiles; they will listen." He lived there two whole years at his own*
*expense and welcomed all who came to him, proclaiming the kingdom of*
*God and teaching about the Lord Jesus Christ. . . . Acts 28:28–31*

THERE WERE MANY who came to Paul in Rome. Some were
driven women, ravaged women, the discontent, the dried-up,
along with doers and dreamers and naive girls who were women
only in their imagined futures. Each one wanted something.
Many of them had been badgered and belittled by men. Most of
them looked ahead and saw humdrum. Everywhere Paul had
gone there were so many scorned, so many "riff-raff," so many
who had been trivialized and dismissed. Paul too had moments
when he patronized and underestimated women. But at his best
he embraced them as disciples, co-workers, co-leaders, equals,
friends. The endless startlement was how easily he grasped the
Spirit's demand that Gentile women too must meet the Christ, be
touched and loved. It was the new way he read Isaiah. It was the
way the many memories and stories of Jesus kept coming at him.

Thus, often the ones who came to this tainted saint in his
Roman chains were women of lack, of need, of heartbreak.
Sometimes they were women of astonishing success and immense
unhappiness. The news they had heard lifelong was impressed
with no-good, and they had been almost convinced of their own.
Then came this one with a gospel of healing and hope. The part of
them that had at moments been stirred by the persistence of olive,
palm, rivulets of water, starshine, breeze, morning sun and how it
could glisten across fields; the part of them that recalled the
laughter of a grandparent, the gentility of a slave, the support of a
friend; the part of them that raged at death and yet at times knew
the eerie sense of some presence, some Other who might stay

with them yet—that fraction of their battered, disillusioned selves made a wide entry for the word Paul spoke. He met them, even as he was housebound and sometimes shackled—with hearty welcome. There was Someone to whom he wished to introduce them.

*God, let us always leave some pathways open into the wilderness of our hearts. Help us all to acknowledge before you our immense need, our unfulfillment, our fragility. We make church, Lord, right where our earthen vessels are cracked.*

## QUESTIONS FOR REFLECTION AND DISCUSSION

Why does it seem to you that the gospel has always—across the centuries—touched with such force those whose hope seems nearly lost?

Given the gospel's appeal to the broken, the desolate, the oppressed, the fearful, and the dismally alone, whom do you see as today's best candidates for receptivity to the Christian message?

# THE SPIRIT PRAYING
### (Read Romans 8:22–27)

*The Spirit helps us in our weakness; for we do not know how to pray as we ought. . . . And God, who searches the heart, knows what is in the mind of the Spirit, because the Spirit intercedes for the saints according to the will of God. Romans 8:26–27*

THOSE WHO HAD SAT along beaches of Mediterranean, those who had watched tides rise and fall, knew that sands dampen, that shells and stones and driftwood wash up with no one's willing it. Those who had lowered themselves into water knew that it held them and that even amid the lap and break of everyday waves they could float.

The Spirit was promised them like steady sea. They did not need to will her washing. They did not need to coax her to be buoyant. They needed only to meet the Spirit as beach meets spray and wader meets water. When surf swelled and waves crashed, they could hold confident. When they prayed, they could swing in and break, at one with tide.

*Spirit of the living God, ease us into oneness with you. As we let our whole selves go, breathe with our breath and rock us in the sea of your immensity.*

## QUESTIONS FOR REFLECTION AND DISCUSSION
The charismatic gift of tongues, the contemplative gift of quiet prayer, the Christian gift of confidence and calm are all signs of our letting go to let God's Spirit overtake us. Why is it that we sometimes find it so difficult to plunge in and let the Spirit work and pray within us?

# CHILDREN OF THE PROMISE
### (Read Romans 9:6–33)

*This means that it is not the children of the flesh who are the children of God, but the children of the promise are counted as the descendants. For this is what the promise said, "About this time I will return, and Sarah shall have a son." Nor is that all; something similar happened to Rebecca when she had conceived children by one husband, our ancestor Isaac.*
Romans 9:8–10

THERE IS A CERTAIN wantonness, a certain unpredictability, in God's will. God's preferences and predilections can make for strange playings out of that divine plan. Sarah, Rebecca, Gomer they remembered—each uniquely herself. Two were matriarchs of chosen Israel, the ancient grandmother and the gold-ringed mother. The other was wife and whore, wooed into deserts, forgiven, and implored as her attention again and again waywarded off. The former two begot the promise. The latter made a prophet whose lavish foolishness was a sign of God's unfailing faithfulness.

Each showed, in her own way, that God would not be foiled and that God's mighty artwork, God's intricate design, was spun of human assent and trust. In the age of the first Christians in Rome, they had to relinquish their narrow sense of Israel and open up their history to others who would embrace Sarah, Rebecca, Leah, Tamar, Rahab, Ruth as their mothers in faith and covenant. They had to widen their hearts to the love-words of Hosea and the benevolent parent, the undying lover, whom he identified as God. They had to stretch their sense of promise around the unexpected Gentiles and know that they too were God's chosen and God's work.

The God of Israel, the God of Jesus, was proving to be wife and mother of surprise.

*Good God, you bring our world around and alter all our history with your unexpectedness. Barren women bear, unknown women become beloved wives, raucous women are pursued, the chosen become suddenly everyone. Help us, God, to be truly, fully catholic—universal in our membership and embrace, adaptable to your widening ways.*

## QUESTIONS FOR REFLECTION AND DISCUSSION

Over and over we find the church remembering. We speak of the Jesus of history as well as the Christ of faith. Why is remembering the Old Testament of such importance to the Christian community?

# PHOEBE THE DEACON
### *(Read Romans 16:1–2)*

*I commend to you our sister Phoebe, a deacon of the church at Cenchreae, so that you may welcome her in the Lord as is fitting for the saints and help her in whatever she may require from you, for she has been a benefactor of many. . . . Romans 16:1–2*

AT CENCHREAE SHE HAD immersed the new women in the name of Abba, Son, and Spirit and lathered them with holy oil. She had shed light on law and prophets as she told the new story and shone upon the faithful resurrection's dawn. She had blessed them all, recalled a holy meal, shared cup and bread.

She came to Rome with Paul's applause. In expansive ways, she had helped so many, he attested. In Rome they could expect her too to minister and serve: to wash them in water and strengthen them in oil, to bear the word with insight, to wait upon the holy table, to edify and inspire, to be sure that all would eat. They would see in her the christened newness of all things.

*Risen Christ, let your life and your word burn within us. Impel us to serve and to make, in many ways, your sacrament of our lives.*

## QUESTIONS FOR REFLECTION AND DISCUSSION

In her book *In Memory of Her*, Elisabeth Schüssler Fiorenza makes much of the fact that Phoebe's role is often rendered in English as "deaconess," while the original New Testament text suggests that Phoebe was a deacon in the same way that any male deacon was. Why might such a distinction in translation make a difference in our interpretation?

Many women worldwide are today doing, in informal ways generally, the things that Phoebe likely did: initiating new members into the church, preaching the gospel with their words and their lives, bearing the gift of Eucharist. What, in your mind, would favor reestablishing the ancient practice of ordaining women as deacons? What might militate against such a move on the part of the official church?

# Mary, Tryphaena, Tryphosa, Persis, and All the Women Workers
### (Read Romans 16:6,12)

*Greet Mary, who worked very hard among you. . . . Greet those workers in the Lord, Tryphaena and Tryphosa. Greet the beloved Persis, who has worked hard in the Lord. Romans 16:6,12*

EVERYWHERE THAT THERE was church, women arose who worked doggedly. They gave their strength to telling the new Way to whoever might happen by and be receptive in the marketplace. They walked from end to end of every city, to villa gates and hovels in crammed alleys, to signal when and where the assembly would next meet, to tend the sick, to see who was in need. They readied a place for worship and, as they always have, did whatever needed to be done to make church work. They were attentive to the elderly and to children, and they heard the lonely hearts' outcry before they ever uttered a word. No detail and no strenuous effort was too much or beneath them.

In Rome there were such marvels. Mary, Tryphaena, Tryphosa, and Persis were among the stalwart women who served the church and seemed to breathe life into the very dust around them.

*Spirit of the Lord, grace us with the gift of attentiveness to great things and small. Attune us to the efficiency that works things well, and grant us the perseverance in the small tasks that let your love be known.*

## Questions for Reflection and Discussion
Among the most overlooked in the church are often the ministers of hospitality. The workforce that talks up and prepares for parish projects and parish picnics, the women who can always be counted on to make things run. Why is it that believers so often

view these tasks as inconsequential, insignificant? What teachings of Paul and indeed of Christ might remind us of the tremendous importance of the efforts of the women on whom every local church counts?

# JUNIA THE APOSTLE
### (Read Romans 16:7)

*Greet Andronicus and Junia, my relatives who were in prison with me;*
*they are prominent among the apostles, and they were in Christ before I*
*was. Romans 16:7*

JUNIA AND ANDRONICUS, apparently wife and husband, were
apostles in the mode of Barnabas, Timothy, Paul, and co-workers
in the expansion of the church as were Priscilla and Aquila. They
were Paul's companions in family and in chains, as we hear from
him. Their lives were lived for the sake of the gospel.

All about the empire, it seems, were women and men whose
confidence and clarity left others shaken. They spoke of their
Christ with authority. Stints in dank, damp prisons and even
threats of death did not daunt them.

There were men who wondered how a woman like Junia might
come by such courage, women who wondered what love this
might be that seemed so far transcending husband-love and family. Her mindset seemed so elsewhere, yet her vision so excep-
tionally present and sharp.

*Give us strength in your Spirit, Lord, to risk because of the dictates of*
*our hearts. Let those hearts always be formed by you, and let our vision*
*be focused on your kingdom—your kingdom as it is, right here in our*
*midst, and your kingdom as it is yet to be.*

## QUESTIONS FOR REFLECTION AND DISCUSSION
Some little bit of scholarly ink has been spilled over the person
of this one apostle and whether the person is Junia (a woman) or
Junius/Junias (a man). Those who argue for the feminine identity
feel some prejudice was at the root of a reluctance to let a woman
be known as an "apostle." Why would it make a difference if a
woman were called an "apostle" by Paul? What did the word

"apostle" mean to him? What does it mean to Christians today?

Church documents frequently refer to the "lay apostolate." In what sense is every member of the church an apostle? Are there certain types of work and activity you would consider "apostolic" and others you would call "non-apostolic"? How would you make the distinction?

# The Mother of Rufus
### (Read Romans 16:13)

*Greet Rufus, chosen in the Lord, and greet his mother—a mother to me also. Romans 16:13*

ANOTHER MOTHER HAD taken a beloved disciple as her son, a mother who had stood beneath a far-off cross. This mother in Rome, like her, knew that there were children everywhere who needed hearty meals, attention, care in their fatigue. She found it to be true even if these children had grown gray or bald, were men with mileage on their sandals and the wear of roads on the hems of their cloaks and robes. She found it when they were women fat with children of their own or gaunt in age and all alone.

Paul regarded Rufus's mother as his own. He knew the church of Rome had found her to be mother too. She was remembered in prayer, in letter, in fond hello. Such mothers made the church who was becoming mother too.

*Christ Lord, your loving mother lives—in her own being and in those mother figures who comfort and strengthen us and urge us on. Let us be mother to one another for the sake of your love.*

## Questions for Reflection and Discussion

Sally Cunneen, in *Mother Church*, observes that effective mothers nurture, encourage, and free. When Paul wrote his letter to the Romans, he acknowledged a mother to him who supported his perilous Christian adventures. How might today's church be *over-protective*? How does it nurture and free people for gospel service?

Identify some contemporary mother figures, those known to the whole church and those who have personally influenced you. What qualities and special gifts do these women seem to have?

Is it appropriate to refer to "mother church"? Why or why not?

# Julia, Nereus's Sister, and Friends
## (Read Romans 16:15–16)

*Greet Philologus, Julia, Nereus and his sister, and Olympas, and all the saints who are with them. Greet one another with a holy kiss. All the churches of Christ greet you. Romans 16:15–16*

A NEW GENIUS, a new creation, came of those early Twelve, those women disciples, those legendary figures and hangers-on who traipsed about Palestine after Jesus the Rabbi. There had been tax collectors, roughnecks in fishing boats, boys with barley loaves, and men who climbed trees. There had been women of means, pale widows, women at wells, foot-washers and prostitutes. This new generation, this Jew and Gentile mix, were being made into church. Male and female, the Spirit recreated them. Those who had seen the Lord—in life or in risen vision—included these new ones among those they called the "saints." Better than any seers or prophets ever had, they knew that saints were ordinary folk with darings and longings, disappointments and dreams, golden moments and desperate failings who let themselves be appealed to and addressed. They were people who could give in and listen. Why? Because the "saints," God's holy people, were simply those who believed well enough of themselves that they could bear a saving word, and who thought well enough of God that they could receive love, even in their incompletion.

*Risen Jesus, draw us into your very being and make us, male and female, into your new creation. Julia and Philologus, Nereus and your sister, all you household of saints, pray for us who remain here, ready for a good word and eager for love.*

## Questions for Reflection and Discussion
While we pledge in prayer, in the creed, our faith in the "com-

munion of saints," we rarely think of either the uncanonized dead or the unhaloed living as "saints." Why was the early church's sense of the "saints" (an expression they used with reference to one another) so much more inclusive than our own? How would it benefit us if we could acknowledge wider possibilities for who the saints might be?

# CHLOE'S HOUSEHOLD
### (Read 1 Corinthians 1:10–13)

*For it has been reported to me by Chloe's people that there are quarrels among you. . . . 1 Corinthians 1:11*

EVEN THE MOST peacekeeping of women could not prevent some among the church that met in her house from resorting to squabbles and tiffs and from rallying around one camp or another. It was some recalcitrance of human nature and some competitiveness that is reluctant to die. Chloe may have thrown up her hands, incredulous. It seemed that some in Corinth couldn't sort out Paul from Cephas, Apollos from Christ. They wanted to be part of someone's following. How long would it take, she wondered, for them to realize that all was Christ? They had the strong words of Paul's letter. She, meanwhile, mulled about the house praying they would praise with one voice again and reverence whatever preaching and baptism had first moved them. To her it seemed so obvious that this Truth they had received, this direction and life-gift, all converged on one, one only, path. The pathway was Jesus, the preaching was Jesus, the baptism was Jesus, and indeed the whole household was Christ.

*Spirit of the one and only Way, as we learn and ally ourselves in you, let us respect our diversity of backgrounds, stories, styles. Let us always look to you and submit to you, who unify.*

## QUESTIONS FOR REFLECTION AND DISCUSSION
Whether we have been refreshed and revitalized in a cursillo, the Blue Army, a charismatic group, a weekend for the divorced and separated, a Bible institute, the Legion of Mary, a school of theology, or in reading the works of our favorite spiritual writer, we all have a tendency to regard the way that has renewed our

lives as the one for everyone. How can we squelch our tendencies to belittle or downplay the many ways other than our own that lead to God? How can we help to build a vibrant church that is truly "pluralistic" in its spiritualities and styles?

# TEMPLE OF GOD
### (Read 1 Corinthians 3:16–17; 6:19–20; 2 Corinthians 5:1–10; 6:16)

*Do you not know that you are God's temple and that God's Spirit dwells
in you? If anyone destroys God's temple, God will destroy that person.
For God's temple is holy, and you are that temple.*

1 Corinthians 3:16–17

THEY HAD BEEN USED to temples as the sites set apart for
burning incense to their hopes and laying down their griefs. They
were accustomed to high and low priests, to holy words, to sacred
bows and gestures, to arcane meanings and unearthly melodies.
They knew of inner sanctums that were inaccessible to the un-
initiated, the unordained, the non-elect.

Now suddenly there came these disciples and evangelists who
broke upon them news that they themselves were temples—that
the Holy of Holies was bright light within them, that the majesty
of God was somehow touchable on their very skin, and that God's
love and wisdom simmered deep in their own hearts and minds.

They themselves were tabernacles worthy of bows, prostra-
tions, genuflections. They themselves were temples before whom
others might make a profound reverence and swing incense.
What was more, they owed a devotion and unutterable awe to
one another. To violate one another would be sacrilege. And yet
they were not to be overtaken by a paralyzing pious fear.

A human mother—a woman whose skin could rash or scar as
readily as theirs, a woman whose eyes could weep and heart
could ache or whose mouth could curve with a smile and break
into laughter as easily as anyone's—such a mother had borne a
son who himself had been shown to be God among them. This
human son—a son who could enjoy or grow angry, eat and sleep,
have hopes and longings, make friends and enemies, be elated or
dejected, feel pain and finally die—this son had proved that they
could triumph and rise. And what they had begun, ever so grad-

ually, to realize was that all this was so only because there was a God who chose to dwell in fragile, flawed, and feckless human flesh. Little by little, it was dawning upon them that there was divine life in their midst, in each one of them. They themselves—whoever—were miracles of godliness. They began to tread more gently and to speak to one another more as they might pray. They suddenly could kiss themselves awake.

*Emmanuel, be born again in us . . . and born . . . and born.*


## QUESTIONS FOR REFLECTION AND DISCUSSION

M. Scott Peck has told the story of a group of weary, jaded monks whose monastery is suddenly revivified when they are told that one of them is the Messiah. They come back to life as they begin treating one another and even regarding themselves as possibly the bearers of this secret identity. How would our Christian lives, our marriages, our family relations, and our friendships alter if we truly—and always—treated one another (and ourselves!) as temples of God?

# Spousal Love
### (Read 1 Corinthians 7:2–4; Ephesians 5:21-22, 25)

*Be subject to one another out of reverence for Christ. Ephesians 5:21*

LOVE, THEY BEGAN to realize, is God's great sign. They began to comprehend more and more its personality and undyingness. Marriage could never again be matter-of-fact, an arrangement of clan or tribe, security for a woman, property for a man, subservience for wife, authority for a husband, the mere relief of night loneliness, or the damping down of a slow burning. No, love became a new way in this faith-life. They began to learn that love is giving over to the loved one, letting oneself be lost in bounty and betterment, laying down one's life, reveling too in being loved, revering God as love's author and only sovereign.

They would be good to one another, rejoicing in love as passionately as the two in Solomon's song, surrendering to love as lavishly as their community broke bread, suffering together as selflessly as each one retraced the road to Calvary. Love means, they learned, a manger bed and an empty tomb. There would be glory and strain from end to end. And the skies would sing as they came to regard one another as body of Christ.

*Let us, O Love, give way within. And make us glad in the loving, the binding, the startlement, the forgiving. Help us always to follow your lead in love.*

## Questions for Reflection and Discussion
What do you consider the basis, in the behaviors and attitudes of Jesus and in the teachings of the New Testament, for understanding marriage as a partnership of equals?

In ecclesiology and in the mystical tradition, the image of the bridegroom and bride has been used to describe the relationship between Christ and the church and between Christ and the individual soul. In what ways do you find the image appropriate? Are there ways in which the image seems inappropriate?

How do you understand the concept of "purity" when it refers to human love?

# BLESSED VIRGINS
### (Read 1 Corinthians 7:32–35)

*And the unmarried woman and the virgin are anxious about the affairs of the Lord, so that they may be holy in body and spirit. . . .*

*1 Corinthians 7:34*

THE EARLY INITIATES in the Way, expectant of a prompt end-time and an explosive second coming, proclaimed that their women and men need belong to no one. It was no disgrace, they taught, for a woman to be her own—to be without spouse and also out of her father's house. It was grace, they claimed, that called some to single-mindedness and whole devotion.

In Christ, a woman's meaning no longer depended on bearing sons to carry on a husband's name. A man's worth no longer was measured in an accumulation of wealth and offspring to last long after him. They had one meaning, and they could rely on that alone. Belonging to Christ, clasping and conforming to him with undivided heart, being seduced and made fruitful by his Spirit: such was their summation. Such was their enough.

*God of all and every love, as lavishly as you bless good marriages, you grant a holiness to loving singleness. Bless the singles among us—those in the workplace, the townhouses and apartment complexes, the charities and the churches, those ordained and those consecrated in community too. Make great lovers of us all.*

## QUESTIONS FOR REFLECTION AND DISCUSSION
Vows of chastity, promises of celibacy, are often viewed negatively in society at large. What often seems to be emphasized is what is given up. How, in light of this scripture and the long history of consecrated virginity in the church, can we understand better the call of some Christians to a committed life of unmarried love?

What ways might the church find to honor more appropriately its singles? What sometimes causes singles who are not "consecrated" or "ordained" to feel like misfits in our parishes? Do you find that most people regard singleness as a "vocation" or as a social role only by default? What attitudes need to change if we are to acknowledge the single life as a unique vocation, as a particular way of loving?

# THE BELIEVING WIVES
### (Read 1 Corinthians 9:1–18)

*Do we not have the right to our food and drink? Do we not have the right to be accompanied by a believing wife, as do the other apostles and the brothers of the Lord and Cephas? Or is it only Barnabas and I who have no right to refrain from working for a living? 1 Corinthians 9:4–6*

BACHELOR PAUL NOTED that Peter and the brothers of the Lord, among others, had their believing women often beside them. It was, after all, within their rights and could have been anyone's. It was indeed faithful and loving. There were perhaps those days when Paul would have wished a wife were tending to him. Yet he also felt there would be a cost to freedom and preaching if he were not, to some extent, footloose and unattached.

The believing women, meanwhile, never had the chance to voice the price they paid in long loneliness, in scrimping and sparse provision, in holding together the home church, in enduring persecution. No one recorded the anguish of their husbands' imprisonments and martyrdoms. No one mentioned their fates. Nor is it ever recalled what pain they bore for their differentness, what ridicule and taunts, what concern for the uncertain futures of their children. No one has reported why they never felt double-crossed.

*We follow in the footsteps, Lord, of ancient, unsung women. Let their silence speak to us, and teach us to remember the gifts they gave. Grant us compassion, too, for the overworked and comfortless heroines and heroes who spread—everywhere!—your name.*

## QUESTIONS FOR REFLECTION AND DISCUSSION
Why is it, do you suppose, that there is next to nothing in the annals of Christendom about the wives and children of the apostles? How do you imagine their lives? How do you account for their silence?

# WOMAN AS EUCHARIST
### (Read 1 Corinthians 10:16–17, 31)

*Because there is one bread, we who are many are one body, for we all partake of the one bread. 1 Corinthians 10:17*

SOMETIMES IT WAS rather casual, sometimes quite ceremonial. But whenever they remembered and made the supper of the Lord, they knew they were bringing their whole beings with the offering. They were blessed, broken, chewed, imbibed, passed to the one beside them. At these moments, they were one. All shades of skin, all semblances of poverty and wealth, all elegance and all ordinariness, all differences of accent, all marks of slavery and freedom, all characteristics of sex, all bearings of health and bendings of illness, all evidences of virtue and remnants of vice—all these pooled together as one blood, all pressed together and warmed together as one bread. No person was superfluous, none superior. Some of them—as some have through the centuries—grasped what it meant.

In their eucharists, the women, with the men, were made receptive. As they accepted the cup, as they consumed the holy bread, it broke upon them that they were opening themselves, their whole beings, both to the somehow present Christ and to the bodies, the lives, the sin, the pain, the triumph, the heartbreak of the entire world. The women's communion was more than a sameness with slaves and Scythians and men. It was a willingness to be overtaken. It was surrender to the entry of Another. It was the patient bearing of the growing frame, the strengthening pulse, of the human race.

Woman knew that she was becoming, would become, Body and Blood, heartbeat and lifebreath, of the universe—if she believed in what she was drinking and what she did eat. She knew she would be swallowed up.

*Lord, we give ourselves over to be your body and blood, your life for the world. Make us aware always of the exaltation and the sacrifice, the splendor and surrender, that you call us to as we become your eucharist.*

## QUESTIONS FOR REFLECTION AND DISCUSSION

The Second Vatican Council, in its *Constitution on the Sacred Liturgy* declared that "the liturgy is the summit toward which the activity of the church is directed; at the same time it is the fountain from which all her power flows" (10). Offer your understanding of this statement.

Traditional hymns and devotions, as well as traditional expressions of the nature of eucharist, have often emphasized the "sacrificial" dimension and have referred to the eucharistic Christ as a "saving victim." Given the fact that there are many reasons today for women to be uneasy with exhortations that they become "victims," is there a positive way in which the "sacrificial" notion can be expressed?

# EQUALS IN CHRIST JESUS
### (Read Galatians 3:25–29)

*There is no longer Jew or Greek, there is no longer slave or free, there is no longer male or female; for all of you are one in Christ Jesus.*

Galatians 3:28

THE PROBLEM FOR the men was stepping from the peg of patriarchy, backing down a ladder rung of ethnocentric or religious pride. The problem for the women was taking in their sudden escalation in esteem and believing—inwardly—that they were as competent, authoritative, certain, wise, talented, and graced as anyone.

Before this Christ, it had seemed that only death, or sometimes catastrophic accident or health collapse, could equalize. Now here they were reconceiving their worth as they began, all alike, in birth and baptism. Life!

The women learned that they were anointed, as greatly so as any male, Jew, potentate, or hierarch. And they were free. They were so by the mere fact of being, by the mere fact of water and God's earth.

*O Christ of all who live, O Christ of time and timelessness, convince us of our inestimable value and our gifts. Exalt our sense of who we are and what we can do—always in you.*

## QUESTIONS FOR REFLECTION AND DISCUSSION

Sandra Schneiders has proposed (in *Beyond Patching*) that original sin may be understood as pride from a male point of view, but that original sin for women may be all that undermines a sense of self-worth, a conviction of personal value, a decisiveness and assurance. What is your response to her suggestion?

Some of the continued discussion of women's ordination in

Catholicism turns on the interpretation and application of this verse (Galatians 3:28). On the one hand is the Vatican argument that the maleness of the priest is an important sacramental sign of the male Jesus. Pope John Paul II has also argued that the maleness of the ordained priest has a symbolic significance when one thinks of Christ as "bridegroom" and the church as "bride." On the other hand is the argument of a number of scripture scholars and theologians that the post-resurrection Christ transcends gender identity—and that we are, after all, in the post-resurrection age. Where are you on the whole question of the ordination of women?

# Freedom, Born of Woman
### (Read Galatians 4:1–7)

*But when the fullness of time had come, God sent his Son, born of a woman, born under the law, in order to redeem those who were under the law, so that we might receive adoption as children. Galatians 4:4–5*

FREEDOM, IN THE END, means knowing that all that belongs to God is also one's own.

The woman who gave birth to the one who secured our legacy as children of earth and assured our freedom as children of God knew how to have everything without holding on. Mary understood that she was daughter of Zion and of Zion's God. And thus she was possessor of all creation. She was free to accept hovel as graciously as palace, a meal of fish and flat bread as easily as banquet, a cup of water as readily as a silver chalice of fine wine. She knew her God as "Abba," provider and progenitor, and thus she could risk her own son's seeming fatherlessness. Somehow she understood that the care of Zion's Abba covered her.

She taught this to her son, who took even the birds and the lilies as his own—without ever having to cage or carry them home. He smiled upon his worldwide inheritance and told everyone that they owned it too. And so they could also let it go.

His mother had shown him the wealth of empty-handedness. Before he was conceived and born, she had already known the lavishness of God and somehow sensed the immensity to which she was heir. Her son brought all his brothers and sisters along into this richness.

*God of abundance and benefaction, give us open hearts to embrace the wealth you have given us. Keep our hands ever open in prayer and in readiness to receive all you pour upon us. And keep them open too for the giving over and the setting free to which your munificence calls us. We revel in your gifts—all your heavens and all good earth.*

## QUESTIONS FOR REFLECTION AND DISCUSSION

In his encyclical *Redemptoris Mater* Pope John Paul II speaks of Mary's identification with the poor among all peoples. He notes that her Magnificat, the song of praise recounted in Luke 1:46-55, reflects "the Christian meaning of freedom and liberation." Indeed, Pope John Paul II says, Mary "is the most perfect image of freedom and of the liberation of humanity and of the universe" (37). How would you explain "freedom" and "liberation" from a Christian (and Marian) point of view?

In 1988 the Catholic Bishops of the Philippines issued a vigorous pastoral letter on ecology entitled "What Is Happening to Our Beautiful Land?" In it they make many concrete suggestions for action and also invoke Mary as "Mother of Life." They sense her involvement in the call to people today to acquire and act on a "vision of caring for earth and living in harmony with it." How do you feel that Mary is connected with ecology?

# EUODIA AND SYNTYCHE
*(Read Philippians 2:12–18; 4:1–7)*

*I urge Euodia and I urge Syntyche to be of the same mind in the Lord. Yes, and I ask you also, my loyal companion, help these women, for they have struggled beside me in the work of the gospel, together with Clement and the rest of my co-workers, whose names are in the book of life. Philippians 4:2–3*

AS CHLOE'S HOUSEHOLD had in Corinth, the church at Philippi knew some unrest. Euodia and Syntyche were tireless gospel workers. Perhaps it was their very ardor that set off whatever quarrel it was that needed reconciling. Paul, who had split with Barnabas, most certainly could understand the situation of two dedicated lovers of Christ who could not see eye to eye.

With prayer, with help, with their own persistence in the one cause that was their life, peace would, however, have to descend on them. Christ too meant accommodation and compromise. Some several styles of preaching, some varied paths of goodness, some different philosophies of operation, some multiplicity of worship and form emerged. The church-in-the-works in Philippi did not count efficiency among its gifts. And it assuredly did not possess a perfect membership. What would make it great would be Euodia and Syntyche's meeting of minds, the gift of a little giving in, without a loss of either's inspiration. What would prosper the church would be the assembly's continued unselfishness in giving them berth, its gift of a loosened grip. The church at Philippi invoked the Spirit's steadying beneficence: breathing space.

*O Wisdom, let your serenity flow over us and let us bring forth nothing but your good. You call us to works of grace. Let us allow leeway—for ourselves and for those who conduct their mission and their lives in ways not altogether like our own.*

## QUESTIONS FOR REFLECTION AND DISCUSSION

It sometimes surprises people that dedicated Christians and even great saints can have disputes and be divided by their disagreements. What causes of contention in the early church do you find still with us today?

# Baptismal Immersion
### (Read Colossians 2:12–15; 3:1–15)

*When you were buried with him in your baptism, you were also raised with him through faith in the power of God, who raised him from the dead. And when you were dead in trespasses . . . God made you alive together with him, when he forgave us all our trespasses. . . .*

Colossians 2:12–13

LEGENDARY SIRENS HAD, for centuries long, been said to lure incautious sailors down to wreck or drown. Now there were these Christian women who plunged the neophytes in, and the neophytes would speak of dying and rising again. The baptized women—and the women deacons who immersed them and gripped their hands as they rose up to where they could breathe air—entered water at a song they had heard from a Creator-God, at a haunting echo caught from Spirit-wind, at a Word who had become their flesh and called it holy. It was not adventure, they said, but their only possible future. Going down in baptism was no ruse to take their breath away and lodge them in some malevolent immortals' mortuary. Letting themselves naked and loose to trust in someone who would baptize them and pull them up was no Scylla or Charybdis. It was, instead, surrender into a tomb that was promised to be empty and radiant with Easter glory.

The baptized women wondered, perhaps, what new strength would be theirs, what glow, what ecstasy. They knew most certainly, however, that no eerie forces, no dissolute spirits, could any longer disarm or dupe them. No evil would or could prevail against them. For they held in faith an apostle's, a Magdalene's, memory. When they emerged from that rippling pool of baptism, they knew that they would discover themselves in a garden. And there One would speak their names and hold them, deathless.

*In the name of Father, Son, and Spirit, we awake to the goodness of life and of our own precious names. Creator, Redeemer, Sanctifier, clothe our new and glorying selves. Keep us, Holy Trinity, ever in your newness, your cleanness, your safety.*

## QUESTIONS FOR REFLECTION AND DISCUSSION
Among the symbolism of water, baptismal garment, the whole ritual of baptism, what elements speak the most to you?

Baptism is always a ceremony of innocence and a surrender in trust. Christians have always held that the sacrament has a lasting impact (indeed leaves one with a kind of "indelible mark"). If baptism is so initiating, cleansing, and definitive, why is it that believers are periodically asked to renew their "baptismal promises"?

# The Christian Heartbeat
### (Read Colossians 3:12–17)

*Above all, clothe yourselves with love, which binds everything together in perfect harmony. And let the peace of Christ rule in your hearts, to which indeed you were called in the one body. And be thankful.*

*Colossians 3:14–15*

SO MANY INFANTS, so many children, had snuggled against their mothers' hearts and been lulled to sleep by the beat. So many athletes had worked their hearts to the utmost pumping, till they became accustomed to muscle and effort and slowed to steady strength. So many lovers had flooded the nights with their pressing, lingering love that the love still echoed on. The Christian heart must be, they reasoned, mother, athlete, and lover. The heart of Jesus had held all of them close, had strained for them, had longed for them and wooed them and caressed them from dusk to dawn, from dawn to dusk. That mighty heart did still. As they caught its tempo, they became reliance; they became peace. The Word rushed into them, and compassion became their lifeblood.

*Sacred Heart of Jesus, let your magnificent love fill us and rule our very beings. Let your kindness and peace pour out of us in kindly attitudes and attentively caring deeds.*

## Questions for Reflection and Discussion

This passage in Colossians speaks of the virtues, the fruits of a spiritual life, as the "clothing" the believer wears. In what sense does the idea of being "dressed" in compassion fit the notion of the changes wrought by baptism and by a faith life? In what ways might the idea of "wearing" Christ fail to communicate the depths of the message?

How do you account for the persistent popularity of images of Jesus' Sacred Heart, First Friday observances, and Sacred Heart prayers? Why does this seventeenth-century devotion still continue to appeal to Catholics? Would you say that this devotion appeals equally to women and men, or more to one sex? Why?

# NYMPHA OF LAODICEA
### (Read Colossians 3:16–17; 4:14–17; Revelation 3:14–17)

*Give my greetings to the brothers and sisters in Laodicea, and to Nympha and the church in her house. And when this letter has been read among you, have it read also in the church of the Laodiceans. . . .*

*Colossians 4:15–16*

THE LAODICEANS, long before they went lukewarm, blessed and broke at Nympha's abode and linked with the Colossian church.

Her house was spacious, as Nympha's heart must have been. She warmed all comers with her welcome, as she spread what rugs and blankets were needed for their sitting when they gathered around her hearth.

Her dwelling had room enough for church and fed its early flame. That was so only because Nympha first had made large heart-room and because her love could take a chance on burning.

*We, Lord, are your dwelling place. Keep us, at our deepest interior, ardent for you, warm and hospitable for yours. Let us always take you in as Guest and blessed guests.*

## QUESTIONS FOR REFLECTION AND DISCUSSION

In Nympha we have another case of a woman likely misidentified in many biblical manuscripts as a man (Nymphas). What cases can you cite where women today are making their dwelling places into church—as parish administrators, conveners of basic communities, lay missioners living in tents or huts, nuns sharing convent space, directors of soup kitchens and shelters, or untitled folks keeping perpetual "open house"? Why is it sometimes difficult to find out about these people?

Why was it risky for women like Nympha to keep a house church in the first-century Greco-Roman world?

# Final Days
## (Read 1 Thessalonians 5:1–11)

*For you yourselves know very well that the day of the Lord will come like a thief in the night. When they say, "There is peace and security," then sudden destruction will come upon them as labor pains come upon a pregnant woman, and there will be no escape! 1 Thessalonians 5:2–3*

THE END-TIME, like so many mysteries, would have, they learned, much in common with the experience of women. It would be like childbirth: anticipated, prepared for, perhaps even practiced or mentally rehearsed, yet fraught with uncertainty, false alarms, contractions, and sighs. And all the while it would still be encircled, for those who loved, with wonder and surprise.

*God, take us through the labor and the splendor of new birth. Show us, in the end, new Jerusalem, new creation, new heavens, new earth.*

## Questions for Reflection and Discussion

A certain fascination with the "end of the world" has persisted throughout the history of Christianity. Why? How do you account for the different notions about it that you can find among Christians from various denominations?

# THE ORDER OF WIDOWS
## (Read 1 Timothy 5:3–16)

*Let a widow be put on the list if she is not less than sixty years old and has been married only once; she must be well attested for her good works, as one who has brought up children, shown hospitality, washed the saints' feet, helped the afflicted, and devoted herself to doing good in every way. 1 Timothy 5:9–10*

LIKE ANNA of Jerusalem, they fixed their gaze on the All-Holy and spent their waking days and broken nights in prayer. Like the loving parent hailed by Hosea, they held and healed old and young, relative and newcomer, refugee and guest. They dipped down deep into the wells that were their store of life-ponderings and drew up love. They lavished it on the parched but also on those whose thirst might well have been, in reality, considerably less than their own. They poured out all they had and testified that God indeed was quenched.

The church assented, and they were honored as weathered and time-tried spouses of Christ. They were supported, blessed.

*God of wisdom, age, and grace, give us reverence for our seniors, for those who have known love and loss. Draw us too into the secret of their survival and their benevolence: the rendezvous they daily make with you.*

## QUESTIONS FOR REFLECTION AND DISCUSSION

Christian history has abounded with stories of widows whose lives were dedicated to the service of the church. Some, like Louise de Marillac or Elizabeth Ann Seton, founded religious communities. Others, like so many of the staunch "inspiriters" and supporters of parish life today, have spent themselves for the church while maintaining their homes, jobs, friendships, and families. Why do you suppose that the fact of widowhood can result in a greater focus on religious and charitable activities for some people? Given the fact that widowhood—or, for that matter, single motherhood—can be fraught with trial and difficulty, are there any positives about it that you can see?

Why do you suppose that in the early church the official recognition of women who were "enrolled" as widows in the service of the church was reserved to women who had reached at least the "mature" age of sixty?

# CLAUDIA, MOTHER OF BISHOP LINUS
### (Read 2 Timothy 2:20; 4:21)

*In a large house there are utensils not only of gold and silver but also of wood and clay, some for special use, some for ordinary. 2 Timothy 2:20*

ACCORDING TO ANCIENT handings-down, Linus, second of those we now hail as pope, was born of Claudia. Rising from raw faith to refinement was as arduous a task as any person could undertake in Asia Minor, Greece, or Rome. To be brought up to shine often meant polishing off status, landholdings, old loves, fond luxuries, safe conduct through treacherous places, leisure, warmth in cold seasons, close-knit kin, well-placed connections, health's ease, attachments to children and even to life. Such things the Christian had to treat, at times, like crust and corrosion. Linus and Claudia were silver and gold. She was one of those women who pooh-poohed the cost. For her, all was Christ.

To the churches elsewhere, elegant Claudia sent hello.

*Lord, give us the grace to give over whatever your good purpose needs. Help us to shed our comforts and securities. And make us lustrous in your service.*

## QUESTIONS FOR REFLECTION AND DISCUSSION
Consider the qualities it takes to live under constant threat. What strengths of personality and belief would a person have to have to be able to let go of everything that is familiar and convenient and even risk the safety of family and self? What convictions or causes would make you willing to risk all that you have?

# OLD WOMEN OF CRETE
## (Read Titus 2:1–5)

*Likewise, tell the older women to be reverent in behavior, not to be slan-
derers or slaves to drink; they are to teach what is good, so that they may
encourage the young women. . . . Titus 2:3–4*

LIKE SO MANY WOMEN who cluster around the worldwide
church, the women of Crete were concerned both with their
standing before God and the public face they wore. On the deepest level was their understanding that being in Christ, being immersed in faith, gave its truest testimony in specific ways of
acting. On a more superficial level, they were aware of general
impressions and public opinion. It would suit them best to be
cooperative, mild, civic-minded, loyal to their families, in-
dustrious, and kind. They were, after all, said to be—and ex-
pected to be—dedicated to Love. And their love was expressed,
rumor said and experience proved, not only in blood-red but also
in soft white martyrdom.

The old women knew that there was both faith testimony and
political impact in their conduct. There must be no slips of
tongue, no off-guard intemperance, no bitterness, no in-fighting;
for these would betray the whole community. They wanted no
one to fault them. Any flaw would reflect poorly, they were sure,
on the very body of the Lord.

And so they told their daughters and their daughters' daughters to be wholesome, exemplary, and circumspect. They told
them to practice quiet strength.

*Lord, never let us reflect your image poorly to the world. Prevent our
giving grist to gossip mills or cause for consternation. Teach us when to
go quietly amid the hurly-burly, and set our sights on lasting things.*

---

## QUESTIONS FOR REFLECTION AND DISCUSSION

When does it matter what other people think? When shouldn't it?

The old women of Crete were counseled to mentor the younger women in caution. The safety of their place and the security of Christians may have depended on some manner of meekness, subservience, silence, and long-suffering. In what circumstances are these qualities fitting and prudent? Where might Christian women be called to be quite otherwise: uncooperative, outspoken, demanding?

# Sisters and Brothers
## at Apphia's Church
### (Read Philemon 1–7)

*Paul, a prisoner of Christ Jesus and Timothy our brother, to Philemon our dear friend and co-worker, to Apphia our sister, to Archippus our fellow soldier, and to the church in your house. . . . Philemon 1–2*

THE COMMUNITY at Colossae, when it unsealed the letter, heard a runaway slave referred to as "brother" and uncelebrated Apphia greeted as "sister." Walls kept tumbling down or breaking through, and the house was remodeled for family room.

It was indeed a new thought and a new thing. Onesimus had been serviceable, strong, and with them long. Apphia was as familiar and presumed upon as walk-worn alleyways or market baskets heaped with more than enough to eat. They had known each other well. But this was an odd twist, this treating each other as kin. A roustabout slave and thief who suddenly believed, after escape, and would be returning politely. A slip of woman who might have been fishmonger, ombudsperson, propertied matron, maidservant, or grandmere. Siblings they now were.

Apphia awaited her brother the slave on the say-so of her brothers Timothy and Paul. The Colossians awaited one another, readjusting their mindsets, as they might smooth wrinkles in cloth. Perhaps, once the idea took, they would even prepare to celebrate a family reunion.

*God, you call us together as one blood, one family, in the name of your anointed one. Teach us to treat one another with love and loyalty, forgiving the offender, gazing again at the one we take for granted.*

## QUESTIONS FOR REFLECTION AND DISCUSSION

Through all the centuries, families have known estrangement. What ways might Paul recommend as the first steps toward mending broken relationships?

There is nothing so sophisticated in the New Testament as a condemnation of slavery, just as there is no proposal for a complete reorganization of male and female social roles. What do we find in the Pauline letters—like this one to Philemon—that might, however, have induced considerable improvement in attitudes and awareness among the Christians?

# A WORD OF CAUTION
## AND SABBATH REST
### (Read Hebrews 3:12–14; 4:9–13)

*Take care, brothers and sisters, that none of you may have an evil, un-*
*believing heart that turns away from the living God. . . . For we have be-*
*come partners of Christ, if only we hold our first confidence firm to the*
*end. Hebrews 3:12, 14*

IF PRISCILLA, or any of the Christian women who had been
hounded and moved around, wrote this letter we call "Hebrews,"
she certainly knew what it was to lose both confidence and heart.
"Fix the vision before you with mystical eyes," she seemed to cry.
"Remember your first love. Clutch him close. Trust his muscle
and sustenance." She knew how tiresome the squabbles, the persecutions, the birthpangs, the changes of mind could become. She
called upon her sisters and brothers to remember their first ardor,
their smittenness with the Risen One, and to stir one another's
memories up. She knew that tired people and those blunted by
troubles could dull their senses, deaden their wits, dupe themselves into easy ways out, and end up dancing with devils.

She reminded them that believers and faithful lovers would enter into God's rest. But first his Word might cut their hearts out.

*God of good rest and timely refreshment, stir us with your oldest stories,*
*and remind us of our falling in love with you. Renew us, restore us, lure*
*us back to confidence and steadiness.*

## QUESTIONS FOR REFLECTION AND DISCUSSION
An immortal work by Dietrich Bonhoeffer tells a story by its
very title: *The Cost of Discipleship.* He speaks often of "costly
grace" and the alteration of one's person that faith must make.
When has the following of Christ seemed to you most costly?

When have you found yourself on the edge of religious fatigue? What, finally, gave you rest?

If we at least nod to the notion that Priscilla and Aquila may have written this epistle, what might you guess about them through their emphasis on sacrifice as they speak of the mystery of Christian life?

A wall plaque that periodically appears on the popular market states: "A friend knows the song in my heart and sings it to me when my memory fails." What connection does this saying have with the idea of Christian encouragement advanced in Hebrews 3:13?

# The Forgiven

*(Read Hebrews 10:12–25)*

*For by a single offering he has perfected for all time those who are sanctified. Hebrews 10:14*

THEY WERE, after all, sparkling. Even if they had nothing to compare with the tales of women with seven devils, five husbands, or wormwood in their hearts, they knew they were immensely understood and forgiven. It had happened in some sense before they were washed with water. It had, in fact, begun when they heard of a man with love in his eyes, warmth in his gesture and smile, healing in his being, and all of God in his past, present, future. He was one who could reach into their hiddenness, their secrecy, and draw forth for them to see a goodness that lay under every disguise and each misstep. His love stretched wide enough to be nailed to torture and death and yet never ceased embracing. As they heard of it and understood, it seemed his love might encircle a whole universe.

Now, after wading into water and being duly drenched, they were sure of it. They had been bathed and cleansed and freshened. There had emerged from within them a beloved, pristine thing.

What now remained was prayer and listening, remembering and alertness, letting live their best and extending the care, the sorority, of counsel and encouragement. There was pool enough for woman after woman.

*Friend and brother of harlots and half-hearts, we thank you for your way of believing in and prizing our better selves. Help us to shake loose whatever remains of old habits and hurts, old haunts and bleak destructiveness, and teach us to see too the brilliance and possibility within ourselves.*

## QUESTIONS FOR REFLECTION AND DISCUSSION

Why do you think that people who have a history of broken-ness and need that has been relieved by renewal or rediscovery feel almost driven to bond with others who share a similar history? In what kinds of groups do you expect to find "recoverers" who minister to one another as "wounded healers"? Do you feel the church itself offers enough support to people who have moved from less-than-best situations in their lives to something better? What more could or should the church do to encourage and befriend people—and women in particular—who are at a point at which they may feel "set free" or "forgiven"?

# FAITH-WOMEN
### (Read Hebrews 11:11, 23, 31, 35, 39–40)

*Yet all these, though they were commended for their faith, did not receive what was promised, since God had provided something better so that they would not, apart from us, be made perfect. Hebrews 11:39–40*

SARAH NEVER SO MUCH as glimpsed the final days, but she saw God's life-giving action. Jochebed, mother of Moses, never, it seems, left Egypt, but she was sweetness and promise in her surviving boy. God grew him up in a papyrus basket and the pharaoh's safety, though Jochebed may not have guessed for what. Rahab knew stories of a dried-up sea and sensed some weighty fate for Israel, though she could not have known why. For no reason but rumor and hunch about whose deity was really Omnipotence, she saved two Israelites and thus her household as down fell Jericho. A widow of Zarephath and a Shunnamite wife received their dead sons back at the words of a prophet, and the mother of the Maccabees let her sons go freely to martyrs' deaths and the afterlife of which she was sure.

The Christians too did not know quite what they would face. And there was very little that was clear about what they were awaiting. What they did know was for whom they waited. And who stood with them in their silent day watches and night vigils.

*God of our elusive destinies, God of all our eternities, stay by us as we live amid the uncertainties of what we do or why. Give us a sense of meaning even when we are unsure of our influence or import.*

## QUESTIONS FOR REFLECTION AND DISCUSSION
In some ways there can be said to be certainties or "guarantees" for the believer: the certainty of God's love, the guarantee of immortality, the undyingness of good. Why, though, do we still at times find it difficult when we cannot see the results of our actions or the fruits of our good intentions?

# RELIVING RAHAB'S RESPONSE
### (Read James 2:14–17, 24–26)

*. . . Was not Rahab the prostitute also justified by works when she welcomed the messengers and sent them out by another road? James 2:25*

IN RAHAB'S CASE, it was the evidence of her well-meaning that saved her. Having good purpose, recognizing the right side to be on, and even believing rightly were all well and good, but the testimony and clincher were the expression, the action. When she put herself out and gave safe-keeping to the clandestine Israelite spies infiltrating Jericho's walls, she showed her mettle. To the new Christians, her old story was clear lesson. One might have been a whore, it said, but God's judgment would fall on how graciously one extended help and succor for good cause.

James was telling them: Like Rahab, we are truly right with God when what we manifest is active love. In faith, the mind assents, the boundaries of the will give in, and the believer surprises herself with the difference her doing makes. The eyes of faith see need. The body of faith responds and feeds and shelters. It may even dissemble for the sake of holy agents.

*Good God in whom we believe, prevent us from ever becoming so relaxed that we become inactive. Let our actions bear witness to our convictions and prayers. Give our faith a human touch and stir our consciences to giving the extra inch or going the extra mile for others.*

## QUESTIONS FOR REFLECTION AND DISCUSSION
Review the story of how Rahab helped the Israelites enter the Promised Land (Joshua 2). Why are she and other unlikely women mentioned as ancestors of Jesus (Matthew 1:5)?

How would you summarize James's perspective on the faith-works discussion relating to "salvation"?

# MILK OF THE SPIRIT
## (Read 1 Peter 2:1–3)

*Like newborn infants, long for the pure spiritual milk. . . . 1 Peter 2:2*

ALMOST EVERY WOMAN knows the need of holding and nurturing. Growth, she knows, can be in adolescent spurts or in the slow gurgle of infancy's hours of sucking, sipping, and sleep.

The Spirit had to feed voracious youths: the new believers who were near-fanatic, passionate, never full enough of the testimonies of Jesus of Nazareth. They reveled in tales and tongues and transformations. They demanded more meaning, more message, more of everything as they dropped their old excesses.

The Spirit had to satisfy too the inquirers who hardly knew whom to seek, what to ask, how to bathe or eat or drink. They seemed slimly aware—and that is all—that they had awakened into something new. And so their sounds came slow; their chubby fists explored thin air.

The Spirit held them all as their old selves fell away, outgrown, and new selves stretched and sprang and flexed and learned to breathe on their own. The Spirit was, for some, the steadiest breast milk. For all, she was the one whose table was always set.

*Pour upon us, Spirit of our Mother-God, a stream of nourishment. Nerve and muscle us with well-being and grow us into goodness and your glory.*

## QUESTIONS FOR REFLECTION AND DISCUSSION

There is an abundance of resources in the church for spiritual nourishment. What particular ones would you recommend for the long-term, well-schooled faithful? What sort of resources would you recommend to the very new member of the church? And what would you suggest as most helpful to the inquirer who knows very little about the faith but has an attraction to it?

What resources have provided the best nourishment for you personally?

# WOMAN AS PRIEST
## (Read 1 Peter 2:4–10)

*You are a chosen race, a royal priesthood, a holy nation, God's own people, in order that you may proclaim the mighty acts of him who called you out of darkness into his marvelous light. 1 Peter 2:9*

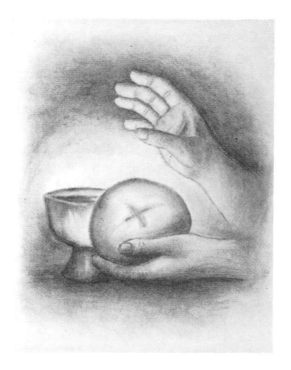

THERE IS A ROYALTY of simply having been born and touching living stone, the women learned. There is a priesthood of all who live, a temple without walls, a Zion without tombs, a church of Spirit-breadth. It would be built on them.

With no sacred smoke, no robes, no special chants, no secret words, the women found themselves, with all believers, ordained of God.

In Jesus' name, in Spirit wind, they sent forth all their lives as sacrifice and sacrament.

Baptism paved their bridge of stepping stones from heaven to earth, from earth to heaven. In their thanksgiving meals and songs, they all—each one—called God to be with them as they offered God-bread, God-wine. At their request and bidding, God bowed down and God rose up to wait upon their table. There God was blessed and broken and breathed upon, and all the guests made God their Guest and found it made them God-women, God-men.

There were sacred words their spirits soon learned. There were ceremonies of birth and mission, of life and death. They spoke the words and made ritual. All the while they remained unutterably new—this priesthood of all who believed, this race of innocents who spoke their peace to God and heard prophecies in their hearts. Nothing but the elements of earth and flesh were needful to vest them. Their very breath became sweet incense. And they were made Christ's pulsing revelation.

*As your priests, O Christ, we speak the minds of all people for your hearing, and we pass on what we receive from you. Make us, in the best way we can be, the bridges between humanity and your divinity. Open us too to see what divinity you already impart to us. And make us sure as stone.*

## QUESTIONS FOR REFLECTION AND DISCUSSION

The Protestant tradition has for a long time emphasized the "priesthood of all believers," and the Catholic church has given the notion of the "common priesthood of the faithful" some prominence since Vatican II. Why do you suppose that this idea of a priesthood of all the people of God receives little attention in our religious education and preaching? How, in Catholic thought, is this priesthood distinct from "ministerial" or "ordained" priesthood? Do you envision a time when, as was the case in the earliest days of the church, there might be much less made of this distinction?

# HOLY WOMEN
*(Read 1 Peter 3:3–6)*

*Do not adorn yourselves outwardly . . . ; rather, let your adornment be the inner self with a gentle and quiet spirit, which is very precious in God's sight.* 1 Peter 3:3–4

THE HOLIEST WOMEN are eye amid hurricane, stillness in squall. So says a letter, in Peter's name, to the scattered churches.

It did not, it seems, mean that the women did not know anger. Nor could it mean that they were strangers to low, depressed pain. But the letter reveals that something in them could triumph again and again. A final confidence. A serenity that seized them and ordered battering, darkness, doubt, fear, anguish to be gone.

In those days the women of the Way had perhaps only begun to grasp where such an anchorhold of strength might come from. There was trust, there was presence, there was future in the Name. The Name, they came to know, was Spirit whispered through them, was Beauty—pure, simple, all their own—spun from and around their hearts.

The holiest women have, the letter tells us, ageless grace. And where it adjures them to "obey," it might equally say "disarm."

*Gentle Spirit, be ours, not just in theory or in wish but in our real responses to the everyday. Settle in us so that we may be settling influences on all we meet.*

## QUESTIONS FOR REFLECTION AND DISCUSSION

Woven throughout the New Testament is the strand of the gentle spirit, the peaceful manner that is meant to be part of the character of the Christian. At times, as in this epistle, it seems that it might be more emphasized as a woman's gift. Why do you suppose that Peter, like Paul in Ephesians, instructs women more to gentility, obedience, and docility, while he exhorts men more to "consideration" (verse 7) and respect? Is there really any difference in the way women and men are called to live their Christian call?

# TRIAL BY FIRE

*(Read 1 Peter 4:12–19; 2 Peter 1:3–11)*

*Beloved, do not be surprised at the fiery ordeal that is taking place among you. . . . 1 Peter 4:12*

SOMEHOW THEY KNEW that all of them, in the end, would be burned. Some of them quite literally torchlit Rome. Others lived on. Some of them, even women nursing newborns, were seared when animals tore their skin in raucous arenas. Others survived them. Some of them were tortured and mutilated. Some of these, along with those left alone, did not die. But all of them were burned.

It was the fire of their vision that kept and browned and lasted beyond them. It was the memory of a Rabbi, a message, a crucifixion, and a morning that flooded Godlight upon them. It was a Pentecost flame that kept flaring up, no matter how many pains were taken, how many threats were made, to damp it down.

The women could not say they were fearless. No. But some things made such a life-difference that fear had to be received and carried. It was rather like taking warm bread from the oven, covering it, and toting it to someone's house or along the street. They ate their fear. They broke it together. There was always more later, and it was always warm.

The women learned that, as with pain, they would never have to carry their fear alone. To lose their fear—their risks, their outcastness, their persecution, their threatened existence—they would have to have lost much more: the thing that had become their very reason for living. A glow that had blinded early Paul, a light that had shone in Lydia's eyes, still illumined them.

And so they remained incandescent. And it would burn them.

*God of light, God of fire, lead us through dark times, doubts, and deprivations. Enlighten us so that we outlive our times and our own lives.*

## QUESTIONS FOR REFLECTION AND DISCUSSION

In what ways have recent martyrdoms of Christians been similar to the ancient ones? In what ways have they been different?

Do you agree that every believer is in some sense "burned" for her or his Christian faith? How do you account for the fact that some people abandon the faith while others hold on?

# THE DOCTRINE OF LOVE
## (Read 1 John 4:7–21)

*God is love, and those who abide in love abide in God, and God abides in them. 1 John 4:16*

AS SPIDERS POUR silky strands of web that weave into artful geometries to catch insects and drops of dew, as bees sweeten bare comb into pools of lush honey, as rose-of-sharon climb vine-like, frond-like, splay-branched and explode into high pink or red or off-white bubbles and open mouths, so love outflows.

The disciples of Jesus, whether the beloved who leaned close to confide in the gentle friend or the devotee who melted to tenderness at the cross and stayed through, with the other women, till the end and then went, all bereft, looking for him in the empty-tomb garden, all of them somehow knew that wonder. They all had fallen into that love that could see through, read hearts, understand, encourage, bless, probe, challenge, forgive, touch their tenderest part. The next generation of disciples found that they could be so caught up and overtaken too. And the generation after. And on and on. Their love made circles of prayer and churches of homes and gospels of fond sayings and twice-told stories and long thoughts, just as it would later make hermitages, leprosaria, mosaics, schools, and plainsong.

The love that Jesus lived and left, the love that was handed on, pressed orphans up to new mothers' breasts, let the fearful and desperate cling close as nighttime siblings, soothed the feverish and sick with basins of clear water and cool cloths, gave to beggars and robbers, kissed the enemy and smiled.

This Jesus whom they had known, whom they had come to know through hearsay if not up close, this Rabbi, brother, mentor, friend, and finally God-man, had poured upon them the lovingness of God, the godliness of Love.

It was not political, administrative, straightforward, or even just. It was not virility, not machismo. It was, rather, artistic, imaginative, senseless, extravagant. It was mercy beyond necessity. It was humanity at its barely comprehensible best.

In the end, this Love they spoke of was divinity with the fondest touch, the widest embrace, the most creative energy.

In this love, Paul waxed poetic, John sang and stormed, Palestrina turned out polyphony, Dante pursued Beatrice all the way to paradise, Michelangelo brought forth Pietà from marble, and millions upon millions of women whose names were forgotten made homes and hostels and hospitals and the fabric of cathedrals as they spent, on person after person, their God-flooded souls. That love that drenched them, saturated them, swelled them, had to inundate the world.

*Ubi caritas et amor (ubi caritas), Deus ibi est . . . we chant and hum in the accents of Taizé's French, the Vatican's Latin, Nigeria's Igbo, Pittsburgh's American.*

## Questions for Reflection and Discussion

When you consider John's famous passage on love (cited here) alongside Paul's famous 1 Corinthians 13, which do you prefer? Why?

In his encyclical on the Holy Spirit, *Dominum et Vivificantem*, Pope John Paul II declares, "Personal love is the Holy Spirit. . . ." (10) How does this statement strike you?

# LADYCHURCH
### (Read 2 John)

*But now, dear lady, I ask you, not as though I were writing you a new commandment, but one we have had from the beginning, let us love one another. . . . This is the commandment just as you have heard it from the beginning—you must walk in it. 2 John 5–6*

IN EPHESUS AND all along mission routes there were nascent churches, studying and straining and trying out, with tentative toes and then certain steps, the way to walk, the way of love. "Elect lady," "chosen lady," "sister" they sometimes called these Christian groups. What were they about, these churches and their children?

They were first of all learning to walk. And the walkway was the path of mutuality, care, acceptance, welcome, compassion, openness of mind and heart. They had the certainty of Jesus' broad embrace. They had the in-gathering of the Spirit. They had the divine life living on. The Christ survived, they memorized by repetition, in the limping simpleton son and the huffing benefactress—who both wanted merely for someone to love them. The Christ reached out in the women who made prayer and shared eucharist in their homes and the men who wandered dusty roads for the sake of the Name. The Christ was roused up in the slave whose soul was set free even while he served and in the destitute young widow who discovered dignity even where she had been groveling.

There were two things they had been cautioned to remember. First, again, that God's love lives; that Love really *is*. Second, that Jesus the Christ indeed had been born a human and indeed had a body yet.

The Body of Love called them to remember flesh.

There would be God in the church as long as there were loaves to eat; as long as oil lathered and hands were laid on the sinful and the sick; as long as there were holy kisses, warm embraces, shoulders to rest on, and sure, safe presences to sleep with. There would be God-with-us as long as voices could speak and hands be raised to bless.

These churches of sons and daughters had new ways of walking—in Spirited bodies, in earthly loves. They were wearing trails for gospels and making blessed oases of roadside pauses. "It is true," the elder cheered them on. "Cling to the commandment. Love the one you see. Love whomever you meet. Treat each as the Christ. For he, for she, is everyone who breathes."

The believers began to wonder if it might not be that walking along with someone, watching with another till calm breath brought heart's ease, was the greatest prayer.

*Lord, teach us to pray. Teach us to stand and walk and stay in love.*


## QUESTIONS FOR REFLECTION AND DISCUSSION

In Hebrew the word for ethics or morality is *halakah*—walking. The "elder" in 2 John commends the "lady" and her children for staying on the path of truth and love. If you were asked to give a simple description of Christian morality, how would you sum it up? What would you call the Christian path or high road, the Christian "way of walking"?

Why does it seem to some people that the law of love is too simple? too naive?

How does 2 John acknowledge that "deceivers" are a threat? How does he advise dealing with those who would deceive or corrupt?

# A Dream of the Second Coming
### (Read 3 John 4–8)

*Beloved, you do faithfully whatever you do for the friends, even though they are strangers to you. . . . 3 John 5*

THE DAY PERHAPS may yet arrive when everyone who meets a journeyer will pause and peer deeply into, and yes will gaze far past, the eyes of the open-handed one who stands there needing something to continue on. The hands of the gazer will fall open too, and both will look intently and see. Both will know that need has met need. And a sudden electric outcry will rise up, "Oh!" And each will know the other to be *pobrito, pobrita*, the living Christ. And the planet will tremble and catch its breath for joy. And everyone will suddenly recognize the person next to her or him. And the stars will sing, and every body cell, every plant, every animal will chorus too, as rock and desert sand tingle and oceans swell. Then the Spirit will know that her fire has caught. Everyone will be going everywhere at the same time. And everyone will be standing still. All will be arm in arm. The embers of homefire will blaze, and there will be time to rest. The Spirit will know it well. She will clap and toss hats and cheer and dance.


*Maranatha!*

*Maranatha!*

# Of Related Interest...

## WomanStory
*Biblical Models for Our Time*
Sister Pamela Smith, SS.C.M.; Art by Sister Virginia DeWan, SS.C.M.
Each of the 56 chapters begins with a Scripture passage and then offers
insightful reflections on a woman from the Bible, her relationship with God and
with her people.

ISBN: 0-89622-460-0, 112 pp, $7.95

## Women of the Gospel
*Sharing God's Compassion*
Isaias Powers, C.P.
Set in contemporary times, this book features 28 women who are being sent by
God from heaven to bring God's compassion to those in need on earth.

ISBN: 0-89622-521-6, 168 pp, $5.95

## A Woman's Healing Song
*Prayers of Consolation for the Separated and Divorced*
Kerrie Hide
Through a series of 12 meditations, Hide offers a thoughtful, spiritual approach
to dealing with the unique grief that comes with divorce and separation. She
uses the writings of Julian of Norwich to illustrate how God's all-encompassing
love can sooth and console.

ISBN: 0-89622-535-6, 80 pp, $7.95

## Women Before God
*Our Own Spirituality*
Lavinia Byrne
This book strikes a unifying bridge between the hard feminist line taken by
some and the traditional approach preferred by others.

ISBN: 0-89622-365-5, 144 pp, $7.95

## Womanprayer, Spiritjourney
Judy Esway
The author illustrates how adversities can become stepping stones to deeper
spiritual awareness and greater maturity.

ISBN: 0-89622-326-4, 80 pp, $4.95

*Available at religious bookstores or from*

TWENTY-THIRD PUBLICATIONS
P.O. Box 180 • Mystic, CT 06355
1-800-321-0411